Advance Praise for *Losers*

"If sports do in fact show us the best of the human spirit, that revelation lies not in championships and victory but in the cold morning of defeat. This book chronicles how human beings respond to failure, how they rise and try again, because that's what living is. It is essential reading—and the self-examination it prompts is essential too."

—Wright Thompson, author of *The Cost of These Dreams*

"Without the threat of loss, there is no meaning in sport. This new and thrillingly varied collection is as essential as the turf beneath your cleats."

—Ben McGrath, staff writer for *The New Yorker*

"Pilon and Thomas explore the significance losing and defeat has on the lives of athletes and fans in this thoughtful anthology. . . . A stirring tribute to losing, one of life's greatest teachers."

—*Publishers Weekly*

"A few of the bylines [in *Losers*] are well-known, especially Gay Talese and Arthur Conan Doyle. Refreshingly, though, most of the contributors are less well-known to general readers, and their subjects range from obscure to famous. . . . As a collection, the book holds together well even for non-sports fans. . . . In the introduction, the editors write, 'This book is for the losers—which is to say, for all of us.' They deliver."

—*Kirkus Reviews*

PENGUIN BOOKS

LOSERS

Mary Pilon is the author of the *New York Times* bestseller *The Monopolists* and *The Kevin Show*. She regularly contributes to *The New Yorker*, *Esquire*, MSNBC, *Vice*, and *Politico*. Pilon has also worked as a staff reporter at the *New York Times* and the *Wall Street Journal* and was a producer for NBC Sports at the 2016 Olympics. Visit her website at marypilon.com.

Louisa Thomas is the author of *Louisa: The Extraordinary Life of Mrs. Adams*; *Conscience: Two Soldiers, Two Pacifists, One Family—A Test of Will and Faith in World War I*; and, with John Urschel, *Mind and Matter: A Life in Math and Football.* She is a *New Yorker* staff writer. Her writing has also appeared in the *New York Times*, the *Washington Post*, *New York*, *The Atlantic*, *Vogue*, and other places.

Both Pilon and Thomas are seasoned losers.

LOSERS

LOSERS

DISPATCHES FROM THE OTHER SIDE OF THE SCOREBOARD

Edited by
Mary Pilon and Louisa Thomas

PENGUIN BOOKS

PENGUIN BOOKS
An imprint of Penguin Random House LLC
penguinrandomhouse.com

Pages 287–88 constitute an extension of this copyright page.

LIBRARY OF CONGRESS CATALOGING-IN-PUBLICATION DATA
Names: Pilon, Mary, editor. | Thomas, Louisa, editor.
Title: Losers : dispatches from the other side of the scoreboard / edited by Mary Pilon and Louisa Thomas.
Other titles: Losers (Penguin Books USA, Inc.)
Description: New York : Penguin Books, 2020. |
Identifiers: LCCN 2019053006 (print) | LCCN 2019053007 (ebook) | ISBN 9780143133834 (trade paperback) | ISBN 9780525505631 (ebook)
Subjects: LCSH: Sports—Psychological aspects. | Defeat (Psychology) | Failure (Psychology) | Athletes—Psychology.
Classification: LCC GV706.4 .L67 2020 (print) | LCC GV706.4 (ebook) | DDC 796.01/9—dc23
LC record available at https://lccn.loc.gov/2019053006
LC ebook record available at https://lccn.loc.gov/2019053007

Printed in the United States of America
1 3 5 7 9 10 8 6 4 2

Designed by Amanda Dewey

It's easy to do anything in victory.
It's in defeat that a man reveals himself.

—FLOYD PATTERSON in "The Loser," by Gay Talese

CONTENTS

Introduction

The locker rooms of winners are crowded. There are coaches, staff, family, friends, and strangers who have managed to slip past security guards; there are the players themselves, who seem suddenly to fill the room more fully than they did before. And there are reporters, flocks of them, ready to record the moment. *How did it happen? How does it feel to be a winner?*

The locker rooms of losers are desolate and awkward. The players are somber, quiet; some shrink into the stalls. People avoid eye contact, keep their distance, as if losing is a contagious infection. There are a few beat reporters on hand, dutifully getting the quotes to file the local story, but they tread carefully and leave quickly, if they're there at all.

That is a mistake.

Victory brings us closer to a fleeting kind of transcendence, but losing reveals something raw about what it means to be human. Everyone—from world champions to the last kid picked on the playground—has known defeat. Yet loss is an intensely private, specific, and isolating experience, ironically when people may need connection and community the most. "I often wonder what other fighters feel, and what goes through their minds when they lose," the boxer Floyd Patterson said to Gay Talese, who is one of the few journalists to mine the rich stories of defeat. "I've wanted so much to talk to another fighter about all this, to compare thoughts, to see if he feels some of the same things I've felt. But who can you talk to?"

So they often stay silent. Yet these are the experiences that may tell us the most. Losing, after all, exposes the dynamics of expectation and pressure in society and reveals the cost of persistence and perseverance. Some have trained their whole lives for a single moment, and they are left with—what? Often a blend of guilt, humiliation, anger, and anxiety. Losing forces a person to account for the past and revise the future. It puts pressure on friendships, coaching relationships, teammates, families. The win that didn't happen can be haunting, making this book, in some respects, a collection of ghost stories. When the pursuit of some goal is gone, people are left with themselves.

The most prominent examples of defeat come, of course, from athletes who seek glory at the highest levels. For some, like LeBron James, who has a losing record in NBA Finals, losses are fodder for arguments about how to evaluate greatness. For others, like Ralph Branca, the pitcher who gave up the home run to Bobby Thomson in 1951 that completed the Giants' improbable comeback to win the National League pennant, defeat is so operatic that it achieves its own kind of immortality. But for others, losing means a kind of erasure. Not many people know the name Jeremy Taiwo, who finished second to Ashton Eaton, the greatest decathlete of all time. For some, like the sailor Kevin Hall, losing can open doors that are long kept shut. Some struggle with a sense of embarrassment or disbelief. Losing, after all, can be taboo—something to be covered up or finessed.

For an athlete, of course, it can be particularly intense, but even fans feel the loss of their favorites with a fierce and personal kind of pain, and even shame. Boston may be enjoying a glut of championships, but for a long time, it was—as its residents knew too well—a losers' town. Likewise Philadelphia, where being a Phillies' fan was, for decades, an exercise in humiliation. For some fans, loss could be even more literal—as fans of Wimbledon FC learned when their football team was sold and moved. And those losses can, in turn, connect to other losses—the loss of a place, the loss of childhood, the loss of a father.

Losses have texture; they complicate. Failure is a fact of life and it is often the greatest teacher we have, yet our most common reaction is to turn away. What if what feels like a loss looks like a win to someone else? What if losing is part of the job description? What if a friend is the one who wins? What if the competition is with a husband? What does winning and losing mean for a sense of one's self?

These essays explore those many questions, and the answers are various. Some of the essays find answers in humor, others through personal reflection. Some are intimately told, while others are told from a distance. There is a story about a marathoner written in 1908, by Sir Arthur Conan Doyle (better known for his Sherlock Holmes series), as well as stories that are still, in some ways, unfolding. They range from Las Vegas to Lyon, from a gymnast from the former USSR to a soccer team from the Ivory Coast. What unites them is their focus on defeat instead of victory. Ultimately, these are stories about resilience, risk, and inspiration, about being knocked down and getting up. We know what that's like, after all. We've lost games, loved ones, jobs. This book is for the losers—which is to say, for all of us.

The Sporting House

CHARLES BOCK

Swee'Pea was his nickname, given to him on the playground courts of New York because of his uniquely oval-shaped head, its eerie resemblance to the baby from *Popeye* cartoons. But in Vegas I never heard him called anything but Lloyd. We said it with force, with a bit of awe. To us, he was *Lloyd*.

I first saw him in the summer of 1986. This was before he got busted at a Vegas crack house, before he got kicked off a college basketball team that he hadn't yet joined, before everything started going to shit and he still was one of the most exciting high school players to come along in years. Summer tournaments were just starting to be a cottage industry, and the Las Vegas Invitational brought in summer-league all-star teams from all over the country, during the stretch of the recruiting season when college coaches were allowed to watch high schoolers play. Games ran from 10:00 A.M. until nearly midnight.

For the most part, the days were desultory, filled with undistinguished action: a backdrop of pounding dribbles, referee whistles, squeaking sneakers, a scoreboard buzzer going a bit too long. The bleachers would be half-filled, some players from the previous game guzzling Gatorade and changing into clean, oversized tees, a cluster of parents at once watching the action and checking to see if any college scouts were watching (and often, during lulls, comparing the merits of various hotel buffets).

But when the New York Gauchos—and especially Lloyd Daniels—played, the bleachers were packed. In fact, bystanders stood in groups in the corners of the court, leaned against the brick walls. At first glance, the Gauchos seemed a ragtag bunch, wearing tight green uniforms the color of well-used pool tables. However, for me, who rapped along to "8 Million Stories" by Kurtis Blow and Run DMC and had all but memorized Rick Telander's chronicle of New York City street ball, *Heaven Is a Playground*, the team's grimy, lackluster attitude only added to my anticipation. Just what had come to us from the mean streets of New York?

I was among the fans checking the names on my folded Xerox of a roster, trying to figure out which dude had been labeled "Magic Johnson with a jump shot," the street-raised hooping genius whose troubles—four different high schools in three states without graduating—had been chronicled in the New York tabloids, the one who'd once defiantly told a reporter, "I ain't allergic to school. I just don't want to go."

Word had spread that UNLV was eager to sign Lloyd—and during one of his last high school games, he'd been photographed wearing Nikes in Rebels red and gray. Though the NCAA forbade brands from sending players sneakers, it was safe to assume UNLV had gotten them into his hands. Jerry Tarkanian—the Rebels' head coach and ruler of the city—had even come down from his throne and was in the gym to watch the game, which didn't happen just because he was interested in watching a high school summer league.

Among the tallest players on the floor, at about six feet eight, Lloyd was lanky. He wore a tee underneath his jersey; short shorts accentuated his angular legs. These days, LeBron James and Kevin Durant have conditioned us to accept huge players in the backcourt, handling the ball, taking charge of the team. At the time, though, basketball pretty much stuck to traditional positions. Lloyd, like Magic Johnson had before him, was the exception pointing into the future. Bringing the ball up court, he'd assume a distinct posture: his forehead tilting downward, chin tucked, eyes concentrating on whatever was happening directly in front of him, his elbow extended like a chicken wing, protecting the ball. His body would be slightly hunched; his head would bob as he moved, nodding along to some internal song. Then he would break the rhythm: a laser pass through an opening nobody else could see; a quick stutter that froze his defender just long enough. He'd cut to the post, take the pass, and in one motion spin and bank in a short shot. He'd push ahead on a break and flip a pass backward without looking, setting up a teammate for a dunk. You could hear the beat of a collective gasp before the crowd erupted into applause.

In the quarter finals, the Gauchos played against a loaded California team whose roster included Chris Mills (who'd go on to spend a decade in the NBA) and Sean Higgins (who'd star on Michigan's only National Championship team). Lloyd was an example of the difference between a prodigy and a genius. There wasn't even a question about who the best player on the floor was. The Gauchos won the game and went on to win the tournament title.

One of my older brothers, Yale, spent that game sitting and talking with the coaching staff from the University of California, Irvine, where he was going into his sophomore year, making his way into coaching by working as the team's student manager. I sat in the row behind him.

I was seventeen, getting ready for my last year of high school. Maybe five foot nine, a buck twenty, one of the five scrawniest kids at Clark High. But I was certain that when puberty kicked in, I'd be playing college ball. Nobody could tell me differently. In lieu of any kind of dating or social life, my days and nights were spent working on my game, preparing myself for destiny: dribbling figure eights and helicopters inside my garage, running sand hills out in the desert, doing calf raises while rewatching college basketball games I'd taped during the season. How crazed was I? Crazed enough that I'd memorized the order of sportscasts on the three local news channels so I could switch around and watch each of their UNLV game highlights, just in case one channel showed a dunk the others had missed.

My parents, because they possessed working eyes, had serious reservations about this chosen path of mine. However, I was in all other affairs unmotivated, sullen, and snotty, and the last thing they wanted was yet another fight with their poor lost child. Thus, when I was old enough to drive, my folks bought me a membership at the Sporting House in exchange for my coming downtown each evening to help them close up the family pawnshop. I soon became a fixture at the Sporting House, my dented, '70s-model Mercury Cougar—nicknamed "the Pissmobile" for its color and demeanor—pulling into the lot amid so many Beemers, Mercedes SELs, and shiny fiberglass Vettes.

The Sporting House was exactly the kind of athletic club you'd expect in our fair, twenty-four-hour city. It was tucked away on an industrial boulevard called Industrial Road, about a three-point shot away from the Las Vegas Strip, and was open around the clock. If that wasn't Vegas-y enough, the place was owned by a snarling middle-aged restaurateur with a pompadour, a permanent tan, and rumors of Mob connections. To get to the Nautilus machines, free weights, stationary bikes, locker rooms, and the private area out back with nude tanning, you first had to pass the sunken, hardwood basketball court, the club's de facto centerpiece—once in a while, you might spot Jerry Lewis or Bill Cosby at the restaurant after a workout, looking down through the huge glass window onto the action. Workday lunchtimes were filled with doctors and lawyer types, who yelled through an hour of full-court. Action picked back up after five, when people started getting off work, and if your squad lost, you'd wait an hour for another run. When the courts weren't crowded, though, I was likely taking jumpers from around the horn, pull-ups from the lane, staring into the wall of mirrors while trying extravagant dribbling combos that almost looked like dance routines. I had a blind faith that this was enough to ensure my future, that I could make it on effort alone.

I'd read that Michael Jordan had asked the University of North Carolina's trainer for baggy shorts because he liked the way they looked, and so I went to Miller's Outpost and bought a few pairs of long surfer shorts to play in. It didn't take long before the House regulars noticed my odd attire and started calling me Maui. That was my nickname—both because of the weird surfer shorts, for sure, and probably also because of the way I played: crazy dribbles, ridiculous no-look passes that rarely connected with their intended target, pulling up for jimmies from behind the pro three-point line like I was high. Or, maybe, because my dreams of becoming legit were obviously implausible. *Maui.*

AS I WRITE, greater Las Vegas has more than two million residents. Ninety-five percent of them will bend over backward to tell you how much the city has changed since the old days (which most of them weren't even here for), how normal its suburbs and exurbs are now. In the '80s, though, even before the hotels had started re-creating landmarks from around the world, the inhabitants knew how the rest of the country thought of Sin City: Sinatra eating poached eggs off the chest of some hooker. People were self-conscious about this, of course. In our fabricated wonderland, we longed for something of our own. But, unlike today's inhabitants, I think we also embraced that outlaw image. *Hey, my cousin poached those eggs.*

Jerry Tarkanian and the UNLV basketball program gave us something successful that was ours *and* something that—like our city, like our way of life—operated on the fringes of rule and law. Or, rather, it had its own rules and laws. Tark came to Vegas in 1973 after a stint at Long Beach State, where he'd become infamous for his willingness to take a chance on players whom—because of grades, personality, or legal standing—other coaches wouldn't touch. Vegas was the city of third-chancers and renegades and black sheep, so it made sense that Tark, with his hangdog personality and his bandit ways, would coach our team. His nickname was Tark the Shark because of the way he famously chewed on a soaked towel on the bench, and, I think, because he was shrewd and daring, a cardsharp, ready to take you for everything you had. His teams played fast and aggressive, the way a team from Vegas should, and within a few years of his arrival the Rebels made it to the Final Four. The newly built Thomas & Mack Center was quickly christened the Shark Tank. When the lights went out for pregame introductions, the student band would start playing the theme to *Jaws*, and a projected shark would circle the rim of the arena. It was all beautiful. Tark had constructed a powerhouse who was guaranteed to make it to the Sweet Sixteen of the NCAA tournament and be in the running for the list of the top high school players in the West. Except the NCAA was after him, big-time. Tarkanian had been at war with the powers that be since his time at Long Beach, when he'd quipped about their hypocritical practices, using different versions of the line "The NCAA is so mad at UCLA for their rule violations, they'll probably suspend Pepperdine for another two years." The NCAA, in return, suspended Tarkanian in 1977—the year of UNLV's first Final Four appearance—charging him with thirty-eight recruiting violations, suspending UNLV's basketball program from postseason activities for three years, and ordering the university to fire Tark. He countered with an injunction blocking the ruling. By the time Lloyd came to town, Tarkanian's lawsuit was on its way to the Supreme Court. Until that got decided, Tark was allowed to coach.

Common sense suggests that the Sporting House—like a number of Vegas businesses—had an unwritten agreement with the basketball program: *We will do whatever favors we can to take care of our guys and keep UNLV winning.* I say this because players, former players, alumni, recruits, and even the coach's grown kids wandered in and out of there all the time. When a Rebel joined your pickup game, it was something of a badge of honor. You ran harder, threw crisper passes, tried to impress with your skills. And on weekend afternoons, the bulk of UNLV's team held court, playing in high-flying shootouts that set the breakaway rims popping.

We gawkers—and sometimes UNLV's coaching staff—would sit on benches, fill the restaurant, which had a view of the court, and line the walkway.

Looking back, I can't help but realize that most of the UNLV players were young black men, and most of the gawkers—most of the club members—were older and white. There were exceptions, but as a rule, the place, like the city's power structure, was dominated by whites.

Vegas has a strong history of segregation. Paul Revere Williams, the architect who originally laid out the development that grew into the nearby suburb of Henderson—a thousand bungalows intended for workers on Hoover Dam—hadn't been allowed to live in the housing development, *the development he designed*, because he was black. Sammy Davis Jr., visiting Vegas as a teenage performer, had been forced to sit in the balcony of the El Portal, a segregated movie theater that also happened to be the only movie theater downtown. Nat King Cole had been physically prevented from walking through the front door of the Tropicana's casino. Indeed, until the '60s, blacks weren't allowed to gamble at any casino or stay in any hotel on the Strip, and instead were directed to the Moulin Rouge, a hotel and casino on what was known as the Westside, a predominantly black neighborhood. Supposedly, Sinatra had a hand in these discriminatory policies being rescinded, but the larger reason things changed involved revenue, not any kind of moral clarity by casino-owning mobsters. In the '70s, North Las Vegas was something like Harlem in the '30s, in the sense that most of the black population lived in a specific neighborhood where street names were just letters and numbers. The black hotel and casino workers would venture downtown and onto the Strip to their jobs. Well into the '80s, it was rare to see a black person on the front page of the liberal *Sun* or the conservative *Review-Journal*—and if a black person made it there, it was usually for playing ball or committing a crime.

There's no doubt that Vegas had more than its share of racial prejudices. I grew up hearing my parents called every anti-Semitic name in English. I also heard racist sentiments emanate from the other side of the pawnshop counter. My dad referred to untold belligerent cowboys as "shit kickers," and my mom let off steam after heated arguments by using the Yiddish epithet for black people, *Schvartz*.

For sure, *I* wasn't racist. Since I'd gotten my license, I'd started driving to the north side of town every two weeks to pick up a new custom-made mixtape from the store where they sold harder-to-find rap records. Hell, I rooted for the Lakers, *despised* the Celtics, wore my too-long shorts. To me, black meant cool, it meant virile—things I wished I could be. When I look back, I see that my *wokeness*, however awkward, was born of a desire for connection. But it was also flawed. Certainly I knew—from PBS documentaries and a short story or two—that the historical fear of black virility and miscegenation had led to lynchings in our country. But did I connect that with my desires? I was aware, to some degree, of societal and financial marginalization based on race, how these core adversities had given rise to so much singularity and depth in black culture. But my teen point of view didn't acknowledge a whole hell of a lot that might exist beyond these surfaces. It was a romantic take on a stereotype.

In eighth grade, our social studies teacher explained that the freeway system in Las Vegas was set up so that when the race wars came, fences could roll down off the side of the freeway to separate the north and west sides of town from the hotels on the Strip, thereby keeping all the gamblers safe.

That's something I still think about every time I'm back and heading toward downtown on I-15.

"YOUR BOY WAS HERE," Charlie Skinner told me. His stepfather was the alleged mobster and Sporting House owner. Skinner, as we called him, was one of the rich kids from the nearby Catholic high school who made up the heart of the larger, loosely assembled group that spent its afternoons at the gym, hustling up full-court games, then bagging on each other over chicken wings and soda in the restaurant. Our abilities ranged. There were talents like the super-quick sharpshooter with white-blond hair who went on to star at the University of Arizona. A number of dudes could legitimately play: I am thinking now of a skinny kid with sensitive eyes and a wispy mustache who happily touched the ball to his knees before dunking backward. Then there were the rest of us. Skinner had some kind of medical condition that forced him to wear heavy metal leg braces when he played. We'd often match up against each other.

Skinner let me know the details of just how Lloyd had *schooled* everyone at the Sporting House the other night. Was it the next day that Lloyd showed up again? His assimilation was that smooth, that natural. He just started appearing at the House, and coming back, always wearing sweatpants, blatantly ignoring Vegas's pounding summer heat, zipping in and out during the afternoon when a lot of us high school guys were playing, sometimes looking for someone, or seeming like he had something going on—*Yo, yo, you seen my man Cliffie?*—but just as often ready to ball, upbeat, with a boyish energy that suggested he was happy to be at the Sporting House, thrilled to be in Vegas, eager to impress, to make good. *Yo, pick sides, let's get it running.* Did any of us know that Mark Warkentien, UNLV's director of basketball operations, had signed documents to become the nineteen-year-old's legal guardian? That the polite, skinny guy who was often at Lloyd's side was a friend of his from 203rd Street back home, and whom UNLV was relying on to keep tabs on Lloyd? That UNLV had set the two of them up in a nearby apartment complex, had assistant coaches bring over a television and dishes, and had also finagled a compact car for him from an advertising company owned by a powerful booster? (This booster was Sig Rogich, an aide to the first Bush White House, and who now has a Vegas middle school named after him.) Did any of us know that Lloyd's mother had passed away when he was four, that he did not know his father, or that his childhood was spent shuttling between one grandmother in Brooklyn and another in Queens? Did we know that Lloyd could read at only a third-grade level, that he was dyslexic and had started smoking pot at nine, that everyone who knew him described him as both a sweet kid and something of a hustler, or that, in response to the question of who his biggest influence was, Lloyd gave the heartbreaking answer "Myself"? Dude was nineteen years old.

This was the summer of 1986. The plan was for Lloyd to attend a junior college in Long Beach in the fall, enroll at UNLV in January, and suit up for the 1987–88 season. A decent amount of this plan actually happened. But if UNLV's coaches, boosters, support staff, and satellite accomplices were all synchronized, working to insure that Lloyd was comfortable and his future safely arranged, then Lloyd—who'd bounced out of two prep schools and between boroughs, and had few skills and little discipline when it came to everyday life—must have felt as if he'd been let loose in a new frontier. And this wasn't just any frontier he was exploring. This was Sin City itself.

We knew none of these behind-the-scenes machinations. We were a bunch of teenagers, after all. So we did what we were supposed to do, as stupid, ball-obsessed teenagers: we shot around with him, rebounded for him, and made ingratiating remarks. We watched him play against other Rebels and talked with one another about how long he'd be at UNLV before he was in the NBA, and about how long it would take him to become an all-star, once he was there. Understand, it wasn't a question of *if* he was getting there.

I once watched as, on his way out of the club to run some

errand, Lloyd nailed a shot not just from half-court, but *from the raised-walkway platform*. Lloyd had moves that none of us had ever seen, moves that reminded us he was from a different world, playing a different game: he had a move where, as the ball rose from the hardwood, he quickly bent his leg and, in a modified soccer move, *dribbled with his knee*, both perplexing and mesmerizing the defender. He also had a jam where he froze you for a second, dribbled through your open legs, and simultaneously raced past you to meet up with the ball on the other side. And it wasn't like he was pulling these moves off against scrubs—he was doing this shit to guys who went on to pro careers. A decade later, these tricks became nationally popular, spreading to pickup courts across the country thanks to And1's mixtapes and subsequent television show. But I promise that not one person who was on the courts with him had ever seen them before. We started practicing them, imitating him. You *gave someone a Lloyd*. You *did a Lloyd*.

In *Swee'Pea: The Story of Lloyd Daniels and Other Playground Basketball Legends*, reporter John Valenti explains that as a child, Lloyd often stayed on the streets deep into the night, hanging out at a Brooklyn playground known as the Hole, as well as a lighted park in Manhattan, near the entrance to the Lincoln Tunnel. Lloyd dribbled off the broken glass in these parks, learning to pass by throwing the ball off the chain-link fence, shooting in the darkness, off the backboard, until he could make ninety-seven or ninety-eight shots out of a hundred.

Maybe this is why Lloyd took pity on me—because he

saw scrawny, outcast, bottom-of-the-totem-pole me at the Sporting House at all hours, putting in work, and it reminded him of a distorted version of his younger self. At least, that's what I hoped, since I wanted to see myself in him. During one full-court run, I was on his team and played under control, hitting open jumpers, making a few smart passes. Who knows, I might even have slapped glass—OK, the protective layer of foam beneath—on a layup. Lloyd noticed, and even learned my name, sort of, not calling me Maui, but Challie, without the *r*, a hard, East Coast–y dialect version, thereby differentiating me from Charlie, which is what he called Skinner, whom, admittedly, Lloyd was a ton friendlier with. I had so little confidence, had so few people encouraging me that, thirty-two years later, I still remember that dollop.

Then one afternoon I was on my way to the Sporting House when I saw, ahead of me, a blue Dodge weaving through traffic. I was in the left lane, about to head under the I-15 freeway, when the Dodge cut me off. It swerved again, jerking into the slightest opening in the neighboring lane, so it could pass one car. Just as recklessly, it swerved back. It was deranged. Then I recognized Lloyd's large oval head. It was both a shock and logical, and also served as a reminder: this was someone I really didn't know.

A lazy afternoon not long after that. The usual high school suspects were on the court, along with a couple of civilians, trying to scrounge up enough people to get a game going. And here was Lloyd, slapping hands, taking a shot from the track just outside the court. More talented guys began to trickle in:

the blond star who'd end up playing for Arizona, the lanky forward slated to anchor the Rebels frontcourt. Obviously, the afternoon was shaping up for serious runs. I could see people lining up at the top of the key to shoot for captains.

I counted bodies, calculated.

If I got into the mix early, set up with the right teammates, who knows how long I could be out there. This was what I was always looking for, working for. A chance to show I could hang.

Showing up now: the affable junior college transfer with a habit of pulling up from five feet behind the three-point line. Now the point guard who'd just set the NCAA record for assists.

Lloyd asked if I was going to shoot. "I have to get to work," I said.

At my parents' store, arriving a solid half hour before they needed me, I went into the back, where I sat at a little desk, read the sports pages, drank Mountain Dew, and cursed my cowardly self. I could not escape the way Lloyd had studied me as I walked off the court. His slight nod had felt like so much more, like he was rendering a verdict upon my manhood. That was the last time he talked to me. Because I wasn't worth fucking with—and we both knew it.

ON FEBRUARY 9, 1987, one month after he enrolled as a student at UNLV, Lloyd Daniels was arrested—for attempting to purchase a controlled substance—as part of a raid on a crack house in North Las Vegas. Video from the raid was televised, and it shows Lloyd, handcuffed, being led into a cop car. He's wearing a gray UNLV sweatshirt and a red North Carolina State cap. His head is low. He looks sheepish and, it's easy to infer, terrified.

It was like a bomb had detonated in the city. I remember a shock that seemed to hit a place deeper than basketball, and that, I think, cut to something fundamental about this city and its residents.

We felt a thrilling pride in the way our renegade town skirted convention; but the flip side of bravado is insecurity. I'd known this since I was a child, when my mother had ordered me: when any teacher or friend asked what my parents did, I was to answer that they were in *sales*.

When Lloyd was arrested, there was that dark thrum of anxiety. The fear that maybe those upstanding bastards were right. Maybe we weren't cutting corners simply because the larger system was broken. We weren't making a grand statement. Maybe we just couldn't play by the rules.

Tarkanian immediately went into damage control, announcing that Lloyd would never play college basketball for UNLV. Lloyd didn't serve time for the bust, but it sent his burgeoning career into a tailspin: he bounced from Vegas to a minor-league basketball team in Topeka, Kansas, then to one in Australia, where he didn't last a season. By 1989, insisting that he just wanted to play ball and make it to the NBA, Lloyd had attended at least two rehab facilities and was living at home in Brooklyn. After scamming a teenager out of a hundred dollars' worth of crack, he answered the front door of his grandmother's home in Brooklyn and was shot three times, one bullet penetrating his right lung, the two others hitting the left side of his neck and his left shoulder.

I was in college when I heard the news. The next day I wore all black. My new college friends, most of whom had made the Division III basketball team that I'd been cut from, made fun of me when they heard why.

During the innumerable hours I'd spent pounding the ball into the hardwood at the Sporting House, it was true, I hadn't recognized the absurdity of my dream about who I was going to become; nevertheless, day by day, I'd been inexorably moving into the person I actually *was* becoming. I still didn't know who that person was. But even if I'd always realized, deep inside, that I didn't *really* belong on the court with the best, I did not want to invalidate all the work I had put into the game, the heart I had invested in my ridiculous dream. Watching Lloyd had been a chance to touch the hem of greatness, to watch the reality of who I'd wanted to be play out. Only it wasn't who I wanted to be, was it?

THE MAN WHO BAILED Lloyd out of jail after that original crack bust in Vegas, back in February 1987, was named Richard Perry. Turns out he'd been banned from college basketball because of his involvement with a point-shaving scandal. In 1991, Perry would be photographed relaxing in a hot tub with three prominent members of the Rebels team, which had finally—*finally*—brought Vegas its long-sought NCAA national championship. It was that front-page hot tub photo that broke the proverbial shark's back. UNLV had grown into the dominant basketball power on the West Coast by then, its notoriety and swag infiltrating the pop-cultural landscape to the point where Tark was the subject of a *Saturday Night Live* skit and Tupac was sporting Rebels gear in music videos. However, there also were signs that Vegas—in a run of ten consecutive years as the nation's fastest-growing city—had started evolving beyond its outlaw image: the FBI was supposedly chasing the Mafia out of the casino resorts; the great Old West gaming families were growing old or getting wrecked by scandal. UNLV's new president, Robert Maxson, had designs on getting the school recognized as more than a basketball factory. Cutting off Tark's juice was a step in that direction. Tarkanian agreed to leave following the 1991 season, effectively ending UNLV's desert dynasty. In the ensuing quarter century, the school has made it to the round of sixteen once, and hasn't been to the NCAA tournament since 2007.

The story wasn't quite over, though, because the Shark swam into the NBA's fresh waters, accepting a job as the head coach of the San Antonio Spurs. One of his first actions—a year after *Sports Illustrated* published a piece titled "Legend or Myth," in which reporter Douglas Looney dismissed Lloyd's chances of ever making it to the NBA—was to sign a married, sober, in-treatment Lloyd Daniels.

Balling with a scar down his right side, and at an estimated

65 percent of his former self, Lloyd began the season as a starter. While an admittedly unmotivated and overmatched Tarkanian was fired after sixteen games, Lloyd played the bulk of two seasons with San Antonio, even filmed a sneaker commercial for British Knights. In this sense, he made it.

But he was never the star we'd dreamed he'd be. It wasn't only the bullets and crack that did him in. He didn't do the weight lifting and conditioning necessary to keep pace with the game. Lloyd bounced around the NBA for the bulk of six seasons as a role player (represented the whole time by a Las Vegas lawyer named David Chesnoff, whom I vaguely remember from the lunchtime games at the Sporting House). In almost every successive year, Lloyd played in fewer games, and anecdotal evidence suggests he exhausted anyone who gave him a chance.

Then again, when you consider that he's the only NBA player who never graduated from high school, and that he had bullets lodged in him to boot, this is still pretty goddamn amazing.

IN 2015, *The Legend of Swee'Pea* premiered at the film festival DOC NYC. Directed by physician Benjamin May, the film looked back at Lloyd's life and also caught up with him as a fifty-something man. Lloyd still struggles with sobriety, which seems to be part of why his ex divorced him. He coaches an AAU team based in New Jersey, named the Lloyd Daniels Rebels (the logo on the team shirts is taken from the UNLV squad). In footage of him coaching, it's apparent that the teeth on the top sides of his mouth are missing. He comes off as simultaneously likable and damaged and angry—someone trying to deal, but not consistently able to cope. Lloyd is described as currently existing hand to mouth, living in motels and on friends' couches. Halfway through the film, Lloyd calls the director and asks him for money. Says his former coach, John Lucas, an NBA player turned drug counselor himself, "Lloyd is running from Lloyd to Lloyd."

BUT MAY ALSO TOOK Lloyd back to Vegas and brought him to the home of an aged, ill Jerry Tarkanian. This took place not long after Tarkanian was voted into the Basketball Hall of Fame but before he died, in 2015. Lloyd's love for Tark and his wife, Lois, is palpable. It's obvious that—as for so many people before and since—his time in Vegas allowed him to ruin himself, but was also filled with as much hope as the man ever knew. It must have been a time when his dreams seemed within reach—or, even better, about to come true. When his real life was about to start.

The last time I saw Lloyd was in the late '90s. I ran across him at the will call window of a Knicks game. I had moved to New York to write; Lloyd was with his wife. He looked healthy, in a designer sweater of striped colors. I introduced myself and mentioned being from Vegas, and noticed his wife tense up, as if just the name meant trouble. Quickly, I said, "I used to play at the Sporting House."

Lloyd's face brightened. He wanted to know about Charlie Skinner.

In later years, I'd be told that Skinner was still in Vegas, that he ran a business that had something to do with tabletop video poker. At the time, though, I didn't know this, and told Lloyd I had no news of our mutual friend. I similarly had no reason to tell Lloyd that the Sporting House had long ago been sold to a national health club chain that had then unloaded it. I certainly didn't say anything about the place's most recent incarnation—I'd actually visited, once, pulling my rental car into that same parking lot, entering the old haunt. It had been a truly surreal experience: on the same spots where I used to practice free throws, and where Lloyd had worked bits of his magic, onetime Russian ballerinas were giving lap dances. Turns out, Club Sapphire advertises itself as the world's largest strip club. I told Lloyd none of this, though. Instead, I wished him my very best, and each of us went off to watch the game.

This piece was originally published in the February 1, 2019, issue of The Believer.

Yankees Strike

BOB SULLIVAN

I was born with a baseball in my hand. I spent my whole childhood as a human version of a border collie, begging to play catch all day long. If I couldn't find a human, I'd find a dog. If I couldn't find a dog, I'd find a wall. Many baseballs sacrificed their lives, as did many brick walls, so I could hurl a ball morning, noon, and night. Of course, I became a pitcher as soon as any Little League team would have me. I lived for the WHACK and puff of dust that flies when a fastball lands just right. Growing up in Northern New Jersey, not far from the town of Montclair, NJ, that Yogi Berra helped make famous, my life's dream was to pitch at Yankee Stadium.

Like 99.9 percent of baseball players, I didn't make it. But I came tantalizingly close—at least vicariously.

Back in 1995, a friend of mine was mere hours away from taking the mound as the opening day starter at Yankee Stadium. His name was Frank Eufemia. I spent weeks giddy over the idea, picking through spring training box scores just to make sure he was on target. Then, tragically, Frank's start was canceled.

All because the Major League Baseball season *wasn't* canceled.

His dream—well, my dream—died. It was murdered by a current Supreme Court justice.

Worse yet, it seemed like everyone in the country was happy about it.

Except me.

THE FALL OF 1994 brought the quietest October anyone could remember. There was no yelling for hot dogs, no arguing with umpires, no collective gasps as fly balls soared into the night. Baseball stadiums were empty; bars had no games to show. Decades of rocky labor relations had finally boiled over, and then, the unthinkable happened. On August 12, 1994, the Major League Baseball season was called off. For the first time in almost a hundred years, there was no World Series. The Fall Classic had survived two world wars, the Great Depression, the gas crisis, all sorts of internal strife. But it couldn't survive this disagreement between millionaires and billionaires.

Everyone lost. Owners lost money; players lost respect; fans lost their summer love. Barbecues lost their soundtrack. Hot dogs and apple pie lost their dinner companion. America lost a bit of its soul.

As the spring of 1995 approached, owners and players weren't ready to settle; instead they seemed ready for a protracted fight. Americans faced the real prospect of no April Opening Day that year. Sort of.

Baseball's owners had a trick up their sleeves. They decided to take a page from NFL owners and their handling of the 1987 strike: they would use replacement players to field teams and start the season. So, in late winter ahead of the strike-ridden season, they began summoning ragtag groups of has-beens and could-have-beens, largely from college ball parks and minor-league stadiums, to Florida and Arizona for spring training. If the players wouldn't settle, the season would begin without them.

At first it seemed like a bargaining gimmick designed to get the players to concede. But as March grew late, and the Grapefruit League got into full swing, it seemed all but certain that the season would begin without the "real" Yankees, or Astros, or Dodgers.

The "star" pitcher of the Yankees replacement team was a former major leaguer named Frank Eufemia. Yes, *that* Frank Eufemia—the same guy who had taught me a sneaky right-handed pickoff move before a game at Hackensack's Foschini Park just a couple of years earlier, when we both pitched for the Hackensack Arrows semipro baseball club.

MY PROFESSIONAL BASEBALL DREAMS had perished years earlier. I didn't have it. I had been just good enough to hang on at every level I played at, until I hit the ceiling right below the pros. I kept reinventing myself, kept learning new trick pitches, trying to keep the dream alive. I played in college, and I played a little after college in semipro leagues. Emphasis on the "semi." Usually, I was a middle reliever, which, until recently, was a kind way of saying I was the last guy on the bench. But I did get to play with, and against, a long list of players who got to The Show. I played against former Red Sox players Mo Vaughn and John Valentin when I was in college. Doug Glanville, who had a great career as an outfielder with the Phillies and is now a TV analyst, played with me on the Hackensack Arrows.

Frank played on the Arrows with me, too.

Most Americans know there's an elaborate system of minor-league baseball teams that feed up into major-league counterparts. They might not realize that there are hundreds of other teams playing in independent leagues around the country. They range from beer leagues up to semipro ball where players are every bit as good as those in the professional minor leagues. Each year, hundreds of baseball players are cut by their pro teams, but they are not ready to give up the dream. They usually catch on with an independent league to stay sharp, build up their résumé, and wait for a phone call.

The calls do come, maybe one a year. Just enough to give everyone else hope.

Frank got one of those calls. In 1992, he was plucked out of our Northern New Jersey semipro league and pitched in eleven games for the New York Mets AAA affiliate, the Tidewater Tides. But he didn't stick, and back he was, playing independent ball when the strike hit.

Frank was much more talented than many of the "wannabe" players who went to replacement spring training that year. In the early 1980s, he had rocketed through the Minnesota Twins' minor-league system ("I left them no choice but to bring me up to big leagues"), and had his major-league debut in 1985. Google him, and you'll find video of him striking out Don Mattingly; a story about him inducing Jim Rice into a double play. His final stats that year were impressive: he was 4-2 with a 3.79 ERA in 39 appearances. He gave up less than a hit per inning and held opposing batters to a .250 average.

But free agency acquisitions and other factors beyond his control kept Frank off the Twins' roster the next year, and soon his path to the majors was blocked.

"The business part is what changes when you get to that level," he said. "That can make it a little bit agonizing and frustrating. But you learn that baseball is a business."

He returned home and pursued a degree in teaching. But he kept pitching, and eventually got that second chance with the Mets. He was thirty-two years old. When that didn't pan out, he figured that was his last shot.

Until the strike.

Legendary New York area sports reporter Bob Klapisch, himself also a pitcher on a New Jersey independent league team, knew the Yankees needed warm bodies and helped make the connection. Yankees General Manager Gene Michael, also known as Stick, showed up to see Eufemia throw.

"Stick was impressed, and I said, 'All right, I'll go down to spring training.' Stick gave me a decent bonus to come down," Eufemia remembers.

Anyone who's ever put on baseball cleats would jump at an invitation to Yankees camp. Frank had grown up in the Bronx watching Mickey Mantle. But this was no ordinary invitation. Frank would be crossing a picket line.

And just like that, Frank was in pinstripes, pitching in "real" spring training games.

"On a sunny, breezy day that was made for baseball, about 200 fans were at Fort Lauderdale Stadium to watch Frank Eufemia throw a strike past Chris Latham to christen the dawning of replacement games," the *New York Times* wrote of his debut.

"I was with five or six other guys with major-league experience. We were all in the same boat, asking 'Are we doing the right thing?'" Frank said. Plenty of journalists asked, too. "I was getting ripped by people like Mike Lupica. I almost coughed up my cornflakes every morning."

One day, then Yankees manager Buck Showalter pulled the "veteran" group aside while they were stretching and offered a quiet warning: "'Why don't you guys get lost today,'" Frank remembers. Word was out that protesters from the Teamsters would be showing up. So Frank and the others didn't practice that day.

"Turned out to be nothing crazy. They just put up a blow-up rat," he said.

Frank understood the situation, better than most observers realized. The previous baseball strike had come in 1985, Frank's only major-league season. Finally enjoying a real pro salary, Frank had just bought a condo when players walked out for two days. It was a scary time for him.

He says he talked to plenty of players during the '95 strike and they didn't take issue with what he was doing. After all, he had learned baseball is a business.

Frank's time staying sharp in semipro leagues paid off. He arrived in Florida ready to impress. In his first spring start, Frank allowed two hits and one run in three innings. By the end of the spring, he had pitched to a 3.95 ERA that spring and was indeed in line to start on opening day.

"Frank has shown us the ability to throw his changeup for a strike in any situation," Showalter said to the *Times*, "and that's important. He's done a good job for us this spring."

I watched all this avidly from my perch as the night sports editor at the *Missourian* newspaper in Columbia, Missouri. I was in graduate school getting a journalism degree, and I helped pay my tuition by running the sports desk at night.

Although the baseball strike horrified me—the Yankees were in first place when the season stopped on August 11—the chance that Frank would pitch wearing the iconic uniform delighted me. By the end of March, there seemed no path for a settlement. The brinkmanship bargaining going on seemed to have no end. It looked like the strike would likely take out the first month or two of the season, and maybe the whole 1995 season.

Then, in fifteen minutes, Sonia Sotomayor dashed my

dreams. In a now-famous ruling, just hours before the "real" replacement games would begin, Judge Sotomayor issued a temporary injunction against the baseball owners, essentially ending the labor fight. She said she didn't need to hear from witnesses, which would have caused a delay (and would have meant the replacement games would go on).

When she was nominated to the Supreme Court fourteen years later, President Obama said Sotomayor has "saved baseball." Maybe. But she also extinguished my last chance at my childhood dream.

Notice I said *my* dream, not Frank's.

As Gene Michael had promised, Eufemia was offered a minor-league contract, but it seemed clear there was no way forward for the thirty-five-year-old.

"I called Stick and said I was going home," he remembers.

HE WENT ON TO baseball greatness in other ways. He led Yogi Berra's Jersey Jackals, playing in Montclair, to the first independent league championship as a player coach. He was the pitching coach at Montclair State University when it won the Division III national championship. He finished his teaching degree and has spent seventeen years teaching at Pascack Hills High School in New Jersey, helping hundreds of young players follow their dreams.

When we talked recently, it seemed I was more frustrated by his near miss in pinstripes than he was.

"When I was done, I was done. I had no regrets. It wasn't

like that," he said. "Maybe if I didn't make it to the big leagues at all, it would have been different. If I died that death as a AAA player knowing I should have been promoted, maybe it would have felt different. But having pitched in the big leagues, and having success in the big leagues, it meant I could sleep at night."

They say athletes die twice, and it's true. At some point, childhood dreams give way to real life. It's true of everyone—some people trade in dreams of working at Yankee Stadium for a real job working at Rockefeller Center, like me, or being a dad, or something else. Eventually, everyone's body breaks down. Life number one ends and life number two begins. Even the winningest athletes eventually lose to Father Time, who is undefeated.

I WOULDN'T TRADE MY career writing books and fighting for consumers in exchange for a few years of playing at Yankee Stadium, but I'd sure pause for a moment to think about it. My baseball life petered out the way most do; the Arrows disbanded and I couldn't find another team to pick me up. Perhaps because I couldn't really make a catcher's glove WHACK anymore by then. But that actually freed me to eventually move for graduate school, and move on with life number two. In some ways, that's what happened with Frank, too.

I did have my moment, however. In my last full season with the Arrows, we had our best team, and we added some talented pitchers, which pushed me far down the depth chart.

I appeared almost exclusively doing mop-up duty, taking the mound mostly to save other pitchers when games were out of hand. I didn't appear in a single meaningful game that year.

Except for the championship game.

We were two innings away from winning our league championship and earning the right to play a regional tournament at the Toronto Blue Jays' AAA park in Syracuse. Baseball tournaments can get pretty hairy, with a lot of games compressed into a short span, and as we fought through a series of tough opponents, the bullpen ran dry. By the eighth inning, with the bases loaded and our pitcher out of gas, there was no one left. No one but me.

Summoned from the pen, I promptly surrendered our one-run lead, but then I induced an inning-ending double play that Arrows players still talk about. It was a rocket line drive right back at me. All those years reacting to bounces off Mount Pleasant Elementary paid off. I stabbed the liner with my glove, perhaps saving my face in the process. I then doubled off the runner at first. We scored in the top of the ninth, and I muddled through the ninth inning to get the last three outs. I got to do that whole throw-your-glove-in-the-air thing as I was tackled by a swarm of men on the field. We then went to Syracuse, and for once in my life, I got to play in a professional baseball park. I immediately bought a Syracuse Chiefs T-shirt. We were eliminated in short order, but I was smiling.

My final pitching won-loss record that year: 1-0.

That means I can sleep at night, too. Sometimes, I even sleep in a Syracuse Chiefs shirt.

Banderillero

BARRY NEWMAN

"Just because your legs is dead don't mean your head is."

—CASEY STENGEL, New York Yankees

Villamuelas, Spain

Soldiers don't start out as generals nor politicians as presidents. In business, managers work their way up. Except for a lucky few, the realization slowly and steadily comes to just about everyone that the top is out of reach.

But bullfighting works the other way around. A bullfighter rockets to the top. From first blush, he is a matador—that bold and arrogant swordsman who artfully entices the bull to its moment of truth. A matador monopolizes the spotlight long enough to convince the world of his incompetence. Then his own moment of truth arrives: the shock of failure and the dawning knowledge that he will never be on top again.

The truth came to Ernesto Sobrino thirteen years ago.

"People stopped taking me seriously," he says, driving his old car through a rainstorm on a Sunday morning, heading out of Madrid and across the Castilian tableland to a bullfight in this little town. He is forty. His chestnut hair is all there, but he appears to have a small pillow under his worn blue sweater.

"Life as a matador became a life of pain," he says. "People made fun of me. Promises were never kept. When I was twenty-seven, I faced reality."

A bull gets dragged to the butcher's after its moment of truth. A matador, if he stays alive and retains some spunk, gets to be a banderillero. That's what Ernesto Sobrino is. So is his friend, Paco Dominguez, who is riding in the back seat. His hair is going, but he wears his jacket draped over his shoulders and carries his cigarette with his arm raised, as if acknowledging an ovation.

"The bullfight is a liberation," he says, blowing smoke into the front seat as the car circles the great stone bullring in Aranjuez. "We risk our lives with joy."

Sobrino pulls out a rag and wipes the condensation from the inside of the windshield. "Paco," he says, "you're a romantic. For me, everything is practical. Gambling with life and death is the way I make money. When you are a matador, you can dream. When you are a banderillero, you have to stop."

Banderilleros are the old men of the bullring. Suited up, these bullfighters look like thick-waisted versions of young matadors. The crowd has a chance to take special note of them when they run at the bull with two barbed sticks and try to place them in its hump before the matador moves in for the kill. A hardy banderillero can keep at this until he is past fifty, although his run will inevitably seem longer every year.

Apart from those two seconds when he places the sticks, the old man's job is to make the matador look good. While the matador struts in front of the bull, taunting it, daring it to charge, the banderillero hovers in the background, an experienced eye on the animal's every twitch. When the matador fumbles, a flick of the banderillero's cape can, by distracting the bull, save the matador from a horn through the thigh and, occasionally, from humiliation. All the old man craves in return is some respect and a day's pay.

Villamuelas appears at the base of a slope: half a dozen streets of two-storied buildings. The bullring is just outside town. It is portable, made of corrugated tin and set up in a muddy field. Spain has fewer bullfights than it did before television and the family car. A banderillero takes what he can get.

"It's your legs and your head," Ernesto Sobrino says as he parks his car in front of the bar in the village square. "You need both. I jog. I don't drink or smoke. The crowd doesn't cheer for me. I'm beyond the point where I expect to be a star. But we are the pillars of the bullfight."

The rain has eased off. A woman is washing out a few things at the fountain. A man is selling fried dough. Strung between two balconies, a banner announces today's fiesta.

The bar is packed, its floor littered with shrimp shells. The band sprawls on plastic chairs, drinking coffee. Men in berets lean on canes, wine glasses in hand. Sobrino works his way through, orders an anisette, then remembers he doesn't drink.

"Just a little," he says. "It warms my stomach. I haven't smoked for a week now." Paco Dominguez lights up. "Must you?" Sobrino says. But Dominguez ignores him—the matador is coming in: tall and svelte, chin held high, hair jet black, eyes hidden behind dark glasses. He is a novice, perhaps twenty years old and, Sobrino confides, without promise.

"A rich kid," he says.

"He comes from a wealthy family," says Dominguez, turning back toward the bar. "His family is investing in him."

"I never had an investor in my life," Sobrino says.

His story is the standard one for bullfighters. He was born in a town like this, left school at eleven, delivered groceries, studied the bullfight newspapers, worshipped Manolete. He walked all night to small-town *capeas*—illegal fights in rings built of boards and parked cars. At fourteen, he stood in front of a bull. At sixteen, he was gored. At eighteen, he was noticed. He dressed as a matador for the first time a year later, in 1961, and killed his first bull.

"I always thought I was good," he says, sitting down under the bar's television, which is showing a bicycle race. "There was one day in Rioja. I had a good bull that day. I mastered it. I was artistic. I cut two ears. For me, this was success. But I don't build sand castles; life proved me wrong."

He sips his anisette, and looks up at the bicycles.

In the bullfight business, the impresario pays the matador, sometimes well. The matador pays his banderilleros, though not always on time and rarely well. As Ernest Hemingway wrote years ago: "There is no man meaner about money with his inferiors than your matador." The banderilleros suffered on. Not until the start of this season did they finally vent their resentment. They walked out.

Their strike lasted a week in March. When it was over, they had won a pay raise of fourteen percent. Now a banderillero gets at least $400 for fighting in a first-class ring. In Villamuelas today, Sobrino should come away with $150. Crisscrossing Spain all summer, he might hit fifty towns and earn $10,000. The extra money will help. But when a bullfight is called off, a banderillero still gets no pay. Nor does he have much of a future once those legs go.

"Money isn't all that important to me," Sobrino says as he drains his anisette. "I'm sincere about that. I'm talking about dignity."

Lunch is ready. The bullfighters and their entourage file past the bar into a bare hall at the rear. A movie screen hangs from the far wall, a stack of chairs in front of it. Two long tables have been set up in the middle of the hall. The matador and his family sit at one. The banderilleros and the picadors, who fight on horseback, sit at the other. So do a few of the impresario's functionaries, one of whom goes by the name of Cadeñas.

Cadeñas is getting old. He has a throaty voice and puffy

skin. When Ernesto Sobrino was a matador, Cadeñas was already a banderillero.

"For thirty-five years I was a bullfighter," he says, spitting out an olive pit. "Now I sell the tickets."

"When I'm through," Sobrino says, "I'd like to be a TV repairman." He takes a sip of wine and looks down at his plate. "The pork is tough," he says.

By late afternoon, when lunch is over, the crowd fills the square. The band plays the *Pasodoble Torero*. The loudspeaker crackles: "The greatest spectacle of bullfighting this afternoon in this wonderful city! Get your tickets now! A sensation!" The bullfighters begin to dress in the bedrooms on the other side of the bar. Then the rain comes down.

The impresario returns from the ring, his shoes muddied. "Impossible," he says. The mayor of Villamuelas steps out onto the balcony of the town hall, overlooking the square, and addresses the townspeople. The spectacular, he announces, is canceled.

Sobrino folds his cape. "A funeral," he says. "We don't get a peseta." He and Paco Dominguez drive back to Madrid to wait for the sun, stopping on the way for another anisette.

Two days later, the sun shines on the fiesta of another Castilian town, San Martin de la Vega. The bullring has been erected right in the square, and the cobbles covered with sand. This ring is dangerous. It has too few places for a bullfighter to hide. Looking less than lithe in his salmon-pink suit, Sobrino is keyed up, his face in a fixed grin.

"Sometimes I suffer so much fear in the ring I don't even see the women," he says, surveying the crowd from behind one of the barriers. As a banderillero, he has twice been seriously gored, both times in the groin. "Every time I get dressed for the fight," he says, "I know it can happen again." He takes a swig from a wineskin and shows his teeth to the fans.

The preliminaries soon end and the fight begins. As each bull charges into the ring, Sobrino hangs behind the barrier, letting the matador who employs him today show off his cape work. On his first run, the banderillero plants the sticks perfectly, without the slightest attempt at pizzazz. On his second, the sticks go flying. The bull wheels and gives chase. Sobrino flees, stiff-legged, over the barrier, with a look on his face of crazed concentration.

It is the only moment all afternoon when the crowd pays him any heed. After his young matador gracefully dispatches the day's final bull, the coup de grâce is left to Sobrino. He performs it with a sharp jab of a short knife, and cuts two ears for the youngster, just as two ears were cut for him on that day in Rioja. Flowers shower down. Sobrino stoops to collect them and presents a bouquet to another novice in his glory.

The bullfighters parade in triumph and disappear beneath the stands. As the crowd leaves, someone lets a spindly-horned calf run loose in the ring. The boys of San Martin de la Vega jump down onto the sand to dance circles around it, acting out their fantasies of becoming matadors someday.

Postscript, August 2018

Life has become only a bit softer for Spain's banderilleros since this story first appeared. In the 1980s, six hundred were serving matadors in the corrida; by the 2010s, the number had dropped to four hundred. As ever, banderilleros get no acclaim. They do, still, get gored. Since the bullfight's birth in the eighteenth century, a researcher has guessed, five hundred bullfighters have died in the ring. Two-thirds died in glory; they were matadores. The rest were banderilleros. In 2016, Victor Barrio was venerated as the first matador to die since 1985. But two unsung banderilleros died, while making their matadors look good, in 1992.

Death, as Hemingway noticed, is what the corrida is about. By some reckonings, its own death is on the way. If TV and the family car once tolled bullfighting's decline, now it's video games, the stars of global football, and campaigners for animal rights. Spain was walloped by 2008's economic crisis, and the bullfight's fortunes fell hard. Yet the ranks of matadorial aspirants grew—a customary resort for young Spanish men out of work and short on hope. As the crisis passed, the corrida ticked up. At the festival of San Isidro every May, Madrid's 24,000-seat Plaza de Toros, Las Ventas, became a surefire sellout. One count has put a year's national attendance at six million.

Is it art? Or a barbaric blood sport? "It is men tormenting and killing a bull; it is a bull being tormented and killed." So wrote Max Eastman in his 1933 review of "Death in the

Afternoon," which led Hemingway to hit Eastman in the face with a book. Asked his opinion in a 2015 interview, Nobel laureate Mario Vargas Llosa said, "It's a very different kind of art because you are playing with your life, with your death, in order to produce beauty."

Most matadors do not die. As for banderilleros, the old man's job has less to do with art than security and maturity. Some still keep at it into their fifties. They make good money, six figures for a few. Their union will insure them against professional "mishaps" (boxing and bungee-jumping specifically excluded). Those who must quit can qualify for disability pay, or might, like Paco Peña, become flamenco singers. Singing, an interviewer wrote, satisfies the same "interior need" Peña once felt "with capote and banderillas in hand."

For all the failures and humiliations, banderilleros usually come out ahead in life. That is not quite the case for every competitor. In Spain's corrida, the real loser, pretty much every time, is the bull.

This piece was originally published in the Wall Street Journal *on June 1, 1983.*

An Athens Odyssey Skips the Medal Mark: Sailing Out of a Square Story

KEVIN HALL

You know the clichés already, but let's rattle them off so that we keep them close.

1. It's about the journey, not the destination.
2. Focus on the process and the result will take care of itself.
3. The important thing in the Olympic Games is not to win but to take part.

I won my first world sailing championship at age sixteen. Before that, I broke records as the youngest person to win a junior singles sailing national title and the first to repeat the feat the following year.

I was the first to switch to the doubles youth division and still win.

Not only that, I won while handing the tiller to a teammate

and learning a whole different skill set as crew: like making the all-star team as pitcher one year, shortstop the next. I became the first to win the team racing national championship four times—with three different teams, no less. I even won a heat at my first Olympic Trials, in 1992, as a middleweight in the heavyweight class. I was twenty-two years old.

All I had to do was keep training smarter and harder, like I always had, and that Olympic medal would be mine one day.

In 1993, I focused on the process—not the result—during my fourth stay in a psychiatric hospital. The first three manic episodes were semiprivate. The fourth one was in front of half the US Olympic team and my coach. Just after that, my girlfriend of four years left like the wind. Suddenly, "the process" started to sound like another excuse. I told myself that I would realize my fourth-grade dream of competing in the Olympics. My declaration became a kind of armor, and I welded it on. Sure, I had been diagnosed with a particularly grandiose form of bipolar disorder and pumped full of drugs, but the voices that yelled "No Excuses!" didn't respond to pills. And sure, I had been diagnosed with testicular cancer not once, but twice, and needed to inject myself weekly with testosterone cuz my balls were in a surgeon's pan somewhere . . . but excuse-ers don't win medals.

No. Matter. What.

Despite. All. The. Setbacks.

That's. Who. I. Am.

Inside me, there was one compass, and it was pointed at survival. Survival started to mean only one thing to me. Survival meant believing and manifesting the story that I could control enough variables and train with enough dedication to compete with enough poise to create enough flow to win the United States Olympic Trials.

I was the guy who told himself every night before bed and every morning on the way to the gym that I was the guy who didn't need the odds in his favor, because I was the guy who would overcome any odds.

1992: 8th

1996: 5th

2000: 2nd

2004: 1st. Olympian.

After twenty-five years of training and four excruciating attempts to win the Olympic Trials over sixteen years, I finally qualified for the American team bound for the 2004 Athens Games.

Mission accomplished!

Now, you'd think I'd be pretty proud at this point. Not only was I on my way to realizing my childhood dream of competing in the Olympics, but it was all after bouncing back from numerous difficult meds changes and eight psychiatric hospital stays. The testosterone battle with the IOC put me on *Good Morning America*. The psychiatric battle was mostly in my head, and never in the media.

There was talk that I should be the flag bearer: How many first-time Olympians were thirty-four-year-old two-time cancer survivors who had battled with the International Olympic Committee for ten years to be allowed to compete despite having no testicles?

Everyone I knew told me that I was already a winner. No matter what happened in Athens. However, there was a big problem. Much of my determination and ability to push out just a few more reps in the gym or drills on the water came from an absolutely-no-refunds buy-in to the narrative that striving to win, and continuing to win, despite the odds, no matter what, is who I was. I had all my skin in that game.

The cost remains hidden until it comes due with a vengeance: anything less than continuing to win can only ever be seen and experienced as failure.

It's not that I underestimated my competition. It's not even that I consciously overestimated myself. It's that my survival had depended for so long on winning an Olympic medal. Or, rather, my survival hinged on my relationship to the story that a medal would fix, heal, validate, complete me. A medal would show everyone how worthy I was. Once they saw that, I could believe them too. A medal would allow me to love myself.

That *complete-me-soon* is the story that drives the leg press up one last time at the gym. That *I'm-worthy-if-I-win* song is the one on the playlist for the extra cycling wind sprints when everyone else is fiddling around with their boat equipment. That *I-will-love-myself-the-moment-the-medal-is-hanging-around-my-neck* belief is the psychosis that drives the inner Ahab to sand and splice and lash while the others sleep.

The week before the Olympics, Coach pulled me aside and told me that my name and story were participating as candidates in the final round of voting for United States Olympic Team flag bearer. The US Sailing Team brass were giddy with the possible implications.

As runner-up flag bearer I was the second American to walk into the stadium in Athens. The jacket with a huge "USA" on the back that I had imagined since childhood was—in fact—a swacket, soft as a lover's sweatshirt. So everything *was* awesome! Stadium flashbulbs twinkled like sixty thousand stars. All those people in the stands, all those flashes. Really? They want to take a picture of me?

The soaring emotions dissolved my reality shield a little bit: *Maybe those grandiose thoughts back in the day weren't as far off as the shrinks said they were. Is there a bigger Show right now on planet Earth? Don't think so.*

Cue dream-come-true music.

This is all for me. They're training me to handle anything. It's not my time yet, and there are bigger stages than this.

Just in front of me, so close I could almost touch it, was the American flag. And this is where it gets embarrassing but oh-so-real about competition and head games: part of me was disappointed that I wasn't carrying that flag. *Runner-up is first loser and first loser is no good. . . .*

Yet another part of me was watching that disappointment and was disgusted with myself about it. The little white letters I was literally carrying on my back on the inside of my swacket, the Olympic Credo itself, screamed that I was already doing the most important thing by taking part. What was wrong with me?

It wasn't all as tidy as it sounds. More the seasickness of mismatched signals as I swayed back and forth between utter elation and confusing shame.

Hey! Begging the mixer to slide the insane clown nightmare vibe down just enough for me to keep it together here.

Fortunately the ceremony was long enough to get my sea legs, and I didn't miss the monumental shared experience of the lighting of the Olympic Torch.

Then the actual competition began. My first start and first leg were excellent. But this was also my first time at the Olympics, and I was playing a game that strongly rewards experience. Slowly but surely over the ten-day competition, I realized that I would not be winning a medal. Then I realized that I had better shift my plan to not losing my sanity. I went into robot-mode autopilot. The opposite of flow.

It hurt, to watch myself from two steps behind. It hurt, to be in the body of an athlete (but in parenthesis). It hurt, to feel disembodied out there on the racecourse. Instead of breath, sensations, sweat, and intuition, it was constant brain-bound conversations about keeping my ship together and why is my timing so off? Very unpleasant. If the goal is to triumph, not just participate, this was not how to do it.

At the Athens Games, I finished eleventh of twenty-five of the best sailors in the world, and I was ashamed.

Shame. Shame. Shame. Shame.

Sorry about that, but I want to you to feel it with me. I

was so ashamed that I didn't sit with my family at the medal ceremony. It's hard to explain, but the gist of the feeling is that I wanted to protect them from the risk of "getting any of me on them." And, I didn't want to have to see the presumed or imagined disappointment in their eyes from so close, so soon.

If I had sailed my best and won the luck lottery that week while a few of the medal favorites did the opposite, would it have been enough to medal? Who knows? I'd been at the game long enough to see stranger things happen. The only thing I knew for sure was that when the racing was over, I had only used all my skill in one leg of one heat.

I led around the first turn of the last race. *Where was that guy all week? Why am I beating myself up now about where he was when I should be racing?* Kinda like the opening ceremony, except the party was over.

When people congratulated me, that hurt too. Either they saw the look on my face and hence their congratulations were patronizing and placating, or—worse—they were genuinely congratulating me for having participated and struggled. I wasn't there for a participation plaque.

I plotted the 2008 quadrennium. I had learned so much. I could do it. I had to do it. I would perish if I didn't do it. My Primary Identity, my Sense of Self and Worth, was at the mercy of this story.

One last try still rang loud in my ears as my partner and I welcomed our first child a few months later. I left the house and my family at 5:00 A.M. every morning but Sunday, to continue my customized Olympic quest training. At 6:30 A.M., I performed an additional program of weights training with my teammates on Emirates Team New Zealand preparing for the 2007 America's Cup.

In my first Olympic event of the new quadrennium I finished second, and I sensed that it was over. I came back from the water each evening to see our son, and I knew deep down that I had to let it go. Right now. Surely I couldn't spend another four years training to be something I had only ever hoped to become at the expense of the father that I had committed to be. I'd be thirty-eight by then.

Less generous but in there somewhere was also this: *Plus, could I bear to lose again?*

Letting go is harder than it sounds: Who am I without my "I'm training for the Olympics to fix myself" identity? What will prop me up if I'm not a good dad? How will I handle not knowing anymore exactly what to do and precisely why I'm doing it?

There's tremendous latitude for self-centeredness as an Olympian in training. We are a bit like the tortured artist. "It's all about me" is widely tolerated as part of aspiring to greatness. But now, without any sanctioned claims to legit excuses, was I just a guy with bad balance in his brain?

Scary stuff. I cried. No Olympic medal. Loser.

Ten years later, I had it all. Three magical children, a healthy partner, a successful and prosperous career, hobbies, even an Olympic key chain that said "Never former, never past." My visible self pretended that I had made peace with it all, or else I wouldn't be using the key chain for the Kia.

It was not over! There I was, watching the 2016 Rio Olympics on my couch at home in Auckland, New Zealand, and sobbing hysterically because I wasn't there. Because I had given up. Because I was a loser . . . oh God! I couldn't even watch the races. I collapsed in shame.

That would have been the time to dig deeper and face that demon, embrace that pain, start a new story, and release that shame.

That's not what I did. I torched the welds of my "Olympian-in-training" armor, only occasionally burning through to the bone. But instead of facing myself in the mirror undisguised and naked, I rigged up a new set. Just as hard and thick, but not nearly as flashy.

I would still win. I would write a book. And once it was written, I would learn to do . . . whatever it is writers did next to win. I was going to win, dammit. No matter what.

As it turns out, writers have the same clichés as athletes. *Listen to your heart. Bring forth whatever is inside you. Write for the writing and the readers will find you.* You know, things you see on cat posters, or that your grandmother might say. I can't help but think of the shiny crab in *Moana* here: "I need three words to tear her argument apart: your granny lied!"

It took quite a while to appreciate that nothing had actually changed. Same discipline. Same focus. Same obsession. Same shell game self-worth shuffleboard baits and switches around process and results. Books and boats both start with "B" . . . and I still didn't know how to *just Be.*

Running sweaty after any finish line seems to promise a pretty good deal. The deal is this: If I achieve enough, it proves that I am OK. Since I have proof that I am OK, I avoid having to love myself, to love myself even if—or especially when—I do nothing. The thing about hitching one's self-image to their athlete-persona's, or writer-persona's, or NBC/XYZ-persona's results is: If you win it's phenomenal and everything is easy. If you don't win, but accept your own excuses, it's not so bad.

Here's the rub: to win at the highest level, you have never, ever, EVER accepted excuses.

It is a long way down from that cliff. And it's not how the rest of life works. It's OK for the kids to tumble out of the minivan into school three minutes late because the oldest was on track to prevail in a subtle boundary negotiation, or the youngest wanted to share her new favorite song on Spotify and talk about how cool the picture of the foxowl with the blue eartips is.

I'm frightened, now, writing these words. The dragon is right here, breathing hot on my neck. I have been sharpening my sword, mastering my ninja creep, for twenty-five years.

(. . .)

(. . .)

I will not share how long the silence was before starting this next paragraph. I will not try to describe the fear. I won't even write about the teardrop on the page.

Dude, you are worthy.

Dude, you are loved.

Dude, you are courageous.

Dude, you win.

And if sometimes you don't win? That's okay too.

(Cue Irish Seafaring Hero Music)

This was the most difficult thing that I have ever written. I know this for many reasons but I will only share this one: by the end of the piece I had to finally forgive, and then love, myself. It occurs to me that this could make me a hands-down winner. This book is titled *Losers*. It was always a trap. What if I couldn't do it? Then what?

"There is no try," said Yoda. Only do.

My name is Kevin A. Hall. I'm a world champion sailor, an Olympian, and a world-champion-and-Olympic-gold-medal-winning coach. I've also competed in the America's Cup as navigator: the one sailor on the boat willing to risk mixing water and electronics. I'm a father of three and a kind and compassionate friend of more. I'm a cancer survivor, and a Heartmind Health Polyphony Voice.

I didn't win an Olympic medal. I'm proud of my accomplishments.

I am getting to know my invisible self. She is very quiet. And very calm. And very wise. She has a long way to go, and heaps of room to grow.

The Peanut Vendor and the Curse

SAMUEL GRAHAM-FELSEN

I came of age in the 1990s—the worst possible timing for a sports-obsessed kid in Boston. The Celtics won three championships in the first six years of my life, but I was too young to remember any of them. Once I was old enough to really care about sports, the Big Three—Larry Bird, Robert Parish, and Kevin McHale—had long since faded. My Celtics were atrocious, a grab bag of listless journeymen, the kind of team that finished seasons with win totals in the teens. They were so unwatchable that their games aired on Channel 68, a basic TV wasteland at the butt end of the dial, featuring *Baywatch* reruns and infomercials. The Patriots of my youth were even worse. The clown car of the NFL, they changed starting quarterbacks twenty-two times between 1987 and 1992. And then there were the Red Sox, the most notorious chokers in American sports, who hadn't won a World Series since World War I. They were almost always great in the regular season, but when it mattered, they never failed to fail. I followed them maniacally.

Like most Boston fans, I bought into the Curse of the Bambino—cast against the Sox in 1918, when owner Harry Frazee sold Babe Ruth to the Yankees in order to finance, of all things, a musical called *No, No, Nanette*—but I believed the Curse extended beyond the Red Sox. Yes, the Curse had certainly caused first baseman Bill Buckner to let a routine grounder roll through his legs in the 1986 World Series, but it had also caused the Celtics' most exciting draft pick ever, Len Bias, to die of a cocaine overdose mere months later, before he'd ever had the chance to don a Celtics jersey. And the Curse definitely had something to do with Larry Bird's prematurely bad back and rapid evanescence, too. (Yes, I had the adolescent sports fan's self-regarding view of a very real tragedy.)

Eventually, I came to believe that my whole city, not just its teams, was cursed—that Boston itself was incapable of succeeding. With its gray skies and rusting overpasses, its chipping triple-deckers and dreary pubs, it seemed permanently mired in submediocrity. To be born Bostonian, I was convinced, was to arrive in the world ill-starred. And in the narcissistic haze of youth, I saw myself as the most cursed Bostonian of all—because, of the dozens and dozens of youth sports teams I belonged to, not a single one of them ever won a championship.

In my backyard, I raged against my fate. A boy alone with a ball, I imagined myself a superstar from some other city. I was Jordan, cashing game-seven-winning three after game-seven-winning three at the buzzer. I was Bo Jackson, up in the bottom of the ninth, two outs, full count, bases obviously loaded, smacking a tennis ball with a jumbo whiffle bat over my neighbor's fence. I'd run around in ecstasy, head tilted to the heavens, making ice clouds with my heavy breath as I feigned the roar of adoring fans.

Then I'd step onto a real field and remember that I was destined to lose. For a tall, relatively strong, not-terrible natural athlete, I was an appalling failure at organized sports. I scored one lousy goal in the seven or so years I played youth soccer—and it really *was* a lousy goal, one of those dribblers that came off the corner of my toe at a fortunate angle. In basketball, my best sport, I routinely flubbed wide-open layups and air-balled free throws. I managed to make my high school's junior varsity basketball squad, even starting in the first game, but within five minutes of that game, after throwing the ball out of bounds or traveling on each of my possessions, my coach yanked me, and I spent the rest of the season warming pine.

Baseball was the worst. I had, conservatively, a .050 lifetime average in Little League. I almost always struck out looking, usually at a safe distance from the plate. At the end of a particularly brutal season, I got a feel-good award from my coach—The Hardest Fought-Out Walk of the Year—which of course made me feel like shit. A couple years later, at age twelve, I experienced the closest thing I've ever had to a panic attack, when, in the playoffs, I was on deck, in the bottom of the final inning, with our team down one and a man in scoring position. My teammate had a full count, and I prayed, frantically, that he would strike out and end the game, so that I wouldn't have to. He grounded out to third. The rest of my teammates huddled in defeat, and I stood off to the side, elated.

The nadir of my Little League life didn't come until my final season. It was 1994, the year of my bar mitzvah, a time when I couldn't have felt less manlike. I played in a league that was dominated by Dominican and Puerto Rican kids, many of whom had been rigorously trained by their dads to become major-league prospects someday; one of the league's star pitchers, Manny Delcarmen, eventually was drafted by the Red Sox and went on to win two World Series rings. Mystifyingly, my coach that season, a surly, middle-aged white guy, chose me for the all-star game, even though I was by far the worst player on my team. I wondered if I was yet again being condescendingly awarded for good effort, or if my coach was throwing racist shade against my far more talented Latino teammates. Either way, I was—everyone knew—the least deserving all-star in years, maybe in league history.

Instead of humanely assembling the all-star squads in advance, a league administrator lined us all up right before the game, and selected us, one by one, in order of talent, for opposing teams. I was, humiliatingly, but understandably, picked last, and when I walked over to my team, one of the league's superstars, a towering Dominican kid, said, "Him?

Man, I *hate* white people." Again, I was humiliated, but understood where he was coming from.

My coach put me in right field, the least prestigious of all Little League positions, to my great relief. I was very happy not to be in the infield, where I might pull a Buckner. I hated fielding grounders, terrified of them after a hard, low drive once bounced up and hit me in the breadbox, knocking the wind out of me. In the outfield, there was virtually no risk of being hit hard by the ball, especially if you backed all the way up to the fence, which is what I did. Eventually, someone hit a soft, blooper fly in my direction. I sprinted toward the ball, my glove aloft, and wildly mistimed it. The ball raced over my head, blipped around the fence, and the batter ended up with a standup two-run triple. I heard grown adults laughing in the stands.

I OFFER THE ALREADY-EXTENSIVE litany of failure above as a way of justifying what is perhaps the most disgraceful act of my life. In that same spring of 1994, during the lead-up to my bar mitzvah, my Jewish Sunday school class took a trip to New York City. The purpose of the trip was to learn about the history of Jewish immigrants on the Lower East Side, to get a sense of where we came from, before being launched into the world as adults. We toured tenements and knish factories and the facades of old synagogues. The whole time, I was tuned out. All I could think about was Canal Street, just a few tantalizing steps south, where vendors were selling the same idiotic tchotchkes and knockoffs they sell to tourists today. My two best friends from Sunday school and I had one feverish goal: to purchase a Yankees snow hat from one of those vendors. Snow hats, which we called "skullies," were cool back then, even in warm weather, and we—three boys born and bred in Boston, boys who would go on to become peanut hawkers at Fenway Park, boys who would become, as was proper for Bostonians, especially ones who worked at Fenway, vicious, unrelenting haters of the Yankees—were convinced that a Yankees skully was the coolest of them all.

This wasn't about the Yankees, who were yet to begin their decade of dominance. This was about New York City. It was the first time we'd ever been there. Its skyline was fifty times bigger than Boston's skyline, which we'd previously assumed, like good little provincials, was pretty big. The World Trade Center was ten times taller than Boston's prime tower, the John Hancock. None of our buildings stabbed through clouds. Boston was a once-great, important city, where big things like the Revolution happened, but it wasn't anymore. It was clinging to long-gone glory; even its skyscrapers were named after wig-wearing dudes who died two hundred years ago. We sensed it before, but we *knew* it now: Boston was a loser city. With Babe Ruth, we'd handed off our potential to be great—not just at baseball, but as a city—to New York. New York was where winning went, and we wanted to win.

On the last day of the trip, we snuck away from the group

and bought our Yankees skullies for five bucks a pop. I don't think any of us had the gall to actually wear these hats in Boston, but from that day on, I privately nursed the fantasy of returning to New York for good.

FROM MY SOPHOMORE YEAR of high school through my final year of college, I worked as a peanut vendor at Fenway Park. Over those seven years, I witnessed hundreds of Red Sox games, thousands of at bats, tens of thousands of pitches, millions of fans walk in and out of the stadium. Each season, I became more emotionally invested in the Sox, and more devastated when I watched them lose in crucial playoff games—almost always to the Yankees, often at the hands of my all-time favorite player, our otherwise invincible pitcher Pedro Martinez. At one point, Pedro even publicly called the Yankees his "daddy." Like most Bostonians, I was outraged by Pedro's admission, but I knew he was right. New York dominated us, possibly always would, and all I—and the rest of Boston—could do was scream, in vain, "Yankees suck!"

By 2003, my loathing of the Yankees had become problematic. I hated their giant salaries and neat haircuts and inhuman unflappability, and I hated their impeccably mannered, impossibly clutch star, Derek Jeter, most of all. In the spring of '03, I traveled to New York to root for the Red Sox at Yankee Stadium and was kicked out for taunting Jeter too aggressively. A few months later, I was kicked out of Yankee

Stadium again—this time, for taunting a child who was cheering for Jeter. From what I recall, each time the kid shouted, "Jeter rules!" I responded, "Jeter *stinks*." I may have said "Jeter sucks." This was a dark period in my life; the details are foggy.

That fall, the Red Sox lost to the Yankees in the playoffs, in the worst possible way. In Game 7 of the American League Championship Series, Pedro blew a three-run lead in the eighth inning. The game went into extra innings, and the Yankees' Aaron Boone, a scrub who'd entered the game as a pinch runner, ended the game in the eleventh with a walk-off homer. I was watching at a bar in Boston with my girlfriend, Sasha (now my wife), who'd grown up on the Upper West Side and was raised as a Yankees fan. I'd converted her into a soft Sox supporter earlier that year. But when she tried to comfort me as Boone rounded the bases, I coldly brushed her off and said something soap-operaish like, "Don't. Just. Don't." I didn't want a New Yorker, even one I madly loved, touching me. I pushed my way out of the bar and wandered into the middle of a busy Boston street, daring the cruel God, who allowed things like Boone's home run to happen, to flatten me with a passing truck.

A little while later, I visited Sasha's parents in Manhattan for the first time. They thought I was nuts. Apparently, upon meeting their closest family friends, who were wearing Yankees hats, I launched into a ten-minute tirade about how much I hated their disgusting, cheating, capitalist pig team, and how they should've been ashamed of themselves, and so on—totally alienating these kind people who were expecting a simple hello. I don't remember this event—probably because this kind of incident was a dime a dozen back then—but for my father-in-law, it's an important part of family lore.

A year passed, and the Yankees and Red Sox were at it again in the 2004 ALCS. By then, I'd graduated from college and moved to New York City to pursue an internship at a film production company, but I held on to my job as a peanut vendor and commuted back to Boston for the playoffs. The Yankees won the first two games at home, and then utterly destroyed the Sox at Fenway in Game 3, scoring nineteen runs. I was so despondent after the Game 3 massacre that I left Game 4 after the sixth inning, which was when vendors were required to stop selling food in the stands. Normally, after I punched out of work, I'd find an empty seat and watch the rest of the game. Not this time. The Red Sox were losing, and I didn't need to see the Yankees sweep them on their home turf.

I was on I-95, driving back to New York City, vowing to never come back, cursing myself for wasting so much of my life on the eternally cursed Sox, when I flipped on the radio, just to check. Dave Roberts had stolen second against the invincible Mariano Rivera in the bottom of the ninth, and Bill Mueller had just knocked him in. The Sox went on to win in extra innings, and then, inconceivably, won the next three games against the Yankees. Like it was an afterthought, they casually swept the Cardinals in the World Series. Just like that, the Curse was over.

I NEVER MOVED BACK to Boston. When I visit now, I see a city full of gleaming glass towers and sleek new waterfront restaurants. There is nothing rusty about it. The "Big Dig," which was a punch line in my youth because no one ever thought it would be completed, is actually done: the tunnels have been built, and the hideous overpasses have been torn down and converted into immaculate green spaces teeming with food trucks. The chipping triple-deckers on my modest childhood block have been renovated and repainted with funky bright colors; they are selling for seven figures. The biotech industry is booming. Young people aren't escaping Boston; they're flooding it.

Since I moved away Boston has emerged as America's dominant sports city. The Red Sox have won three more World Series. The Celtics added their record seventeenth championship banner in 2008. The Bruins brought home a Stanley Cup in 2011. And the Patriots have become one of the greatest franchises in the history of any sport, anywhere, reaching the Super Bowl nine times since 2001, winning it six times. Nobody talks about the Curse anymore; I wonder how many Bostonians even remember it.

I will always root for Boston teams, but each year, I find myself cheering with less and less fervor. There's something about all this winning that doesn't sit well with me, something that makes me feel overstuffed as a fan. The more Boston thrives, the more I miss the city that my childhood self was so exasperated by. I miss being from a place defined by its hatred of its superiors, not by its smug dominion over its inferiors. I miss my sad, postprime Celtics and long-suffering Sox. I miss the tragicomic city I knew, the Boston that was a loser.

That Loser LeBron

RYAN O'HANLON

LeBron James was always going to lose, and it was Michael Jordan's fault. In LeBron's first *Sports Illustrated* cover story in 2002, an iconic mouth-agape image from his high school days—an Edvard Munch rendering of a McDonald's All-American—Michael Jordan's name is mentioned nineteen different times. The story begins with a scene featuring Jordan and ends with the image of a fake magazine cover sitting above the television in LeBron's apartment, featuring his photograph and the headline, "IS HE THE NEXT MICHAEL JORDAN?" What made Jordan *Jordan*, of course, was that Jordan always won: six titles in six tries.

That perfect record in the NBA Finals created an airtight mystique around Jordan. He turned basketball, a dynamic team game between ten players forced into constant motion in an effort to create or deny space, into a zero-sum battle for individual supremacy. Watch any of his highlight reels, and you won't see clips of Jordan following the patterns of a preplanned play. You'll see him soaring above the typical constraints of the game, both physically and philosophically. He didn't lead his teammates, so much as he pummeled them into submission. (He once punched Steve Kerr in the face during a practice, and Kerr, who's now won three titles as head coach of the Golden State Warriors, has since referred to the incident as "one of the best things that ever happened for me.") Watching Jordan's Bulls in the NBA Finals, it *never* felt like they would lose because Jordan had redefined the terms of basketball: nobody was better than Michael Jordan, and Jordan proved he was the best because his teams won.

Then came LeBron, loser of six of the nine NBA Finals that he's played in.

The 2015 NBA Finals: the moment LeBron James cemented his particular legend. His team, the Cleveland Cavaliers, had finished the previous season, playing without him, well short of a playoff berth, with just 33 wins in 82 games, near the bottom of the league. James, in his return to his home state, to the team that had drafted him, took the Cavs to the doorstep of its first-ever title. But Kevin Love, the superstar big man acquired from the Minnesota Timberwolves soon after James rejoined Cleveland, dislocated his shoulder against the Boston Celtics in the first round of the playoffs. And then Kyrie Irving, the improvisational whiz kid and the face of the sad pre-post-James Cavs, fractured his kneecap in Game 1 of the finals. So LeBron would have to do it alone.

And he would have to do it by bucking the way basketball was supposed to be played now. The year before, the San Antonio Spurs won the title with a freewheeling, ball-sharing style—what ESPN's Jackie MacMullan called "a symphony of cutting and dribbling and passing and scoring." And Cleveland's opponent in 2015, the Warriors, were the lodestar for basketball's latest revolution: constant ball movement, positional flexibility, and an obsession with only taking efficient shots (at the rim or behind the three-point arc). What the Cavs were playing was almost a primal form of basketball—reminiscent of the ancient glory days of the Jordan Bulls, in the 1990s: give the ball to your best player, let him pound the air out of each possession, trust him to make the right decision as the shot clock ticks toward zero, and then do it again, every single time. During the series, Cavs head coach David Blatt was asked about the LeBron-centric approach. "Could this be sustained?" he said. "No. Nor would we want it to be."

Cleveland took a 2–1 series lead, before Golden State made a key lineup adjustment and won the next three games to clinch the title. James finished the series as the only player in NBA history to lead all players in the finals in points, rebounds, and assists. Add up his per game averages in each of those categories and you get 58; no other player in league history has eclipsed 57 in the finals. Per this rudimentary metric, which was developed by *FiveThirtyEight*'s Neil Paine, the eight players behind James all won both the championship and finals MVP. He lost.

James, of course, would win the title the next year, over the Warriors, the best regular-season NBA team in history. And he won that title for the fans who burned his jersey and the owner who called his initial departure from the Cavaliers—immortalized in The Decision, the clumsy, televised announcement that he'd be "taking my talents to South Beach" to play for the Miami Heat—a "cowardly betrayal."

But then came eight more lost games during the finals against Golden State over the next two seasons, before LeBron departed for Los Angeles, land of . . . the losers. Below LeBron on the list of the most games lost in the NBA Finals: Elgin Baylor, Kareem Abdul-Jabbar, and Magic Johnson—three Hall of Famers with forty-two NBA All-Star Game appearances between them.

It's certainly odd that James, by far the best player of his generation and arguably the most-talented player of all time, has lost twice as many finals series as he's won. That would seem to either negate LeBron's claim for supremacy or falsify the logic of the Jordan era that the best player always wins. More than anything, though, it speaks to how much basketball has changed in the years since Jordan retired.

Today, teams constantly push the ball up the court in an effort to attack unsettled defenses. If they can't find an easy shot and have to work against a packed-in defense, they'll spread all their players around the three-point arc in an effort to create room for the most efficient shots possible. The style, now near universal, has become known as "pace and space." In Jordan's last season with Chicago, NBA teams averaged around 90 possessions per game; in 2017-18, that number rose to 97. Efficiency has also skyrocketed: the league-wide effective field-goal percentage, which adjusts for the fact that three-pointers are worth more than two-pointers, was .478 in 1997-98, and ten years later it was all the way up to .519.

Front offices now have employees strictly dedicated to navigating the peculiarities of the salary cap or developing new analytical models for understanding the game. The individualistic game that defined Jordan's era has given way to a version of the sport that requires interplay from all five players and expects them all to contribute and fit into multiple roles over the course of a single game, quarter, or possession. In the playoffs, if there's one below-average defender or shooter on the court, teams will exploit that advantage until the player is essentially shamed to the bench. Teams are being built, both on and off the court, with ultimate efficiency as the guiding principle.

It would be easy to assume that LeBron, with his singular ability to take over and dominate a game by himself, stands in opposition to this trend. But in fact, he embodies it. While Jordan always seemed to rise above what was happening on the court, James seems to exist directly at the core of it. For all his physical gifts—he's the size of an oil tanker and has the muscle density of a collapsed neutron star, and yet he moves with the graceful pace of a speed skater—what truly makes him stand out is what often feels like a psychic understanding of the flow of the game. It's as if he sees the end of a play not just while it's in motion, but before it even starts.

"I'm lucky to have a photographic memory . . . and to have learned how to work with it," James once told ESPN's Brian Windhorst. With his physical versatility and mental omnipotence, James can cycle through being a creator, scorer, rebounder, pick-setter on one end and then guard a center and a point guard on the other.

The best teams in the NBA are now essentially built in the adaptable image of the league's best player. Those 2015 NBA Finals turned on Kerr's decision to switch to what became known as the "Death Lineup," a group without a traditional center, surrounding point guard Stephen Curry with four wing players who could rotate around the perimeter and all hit open shots. They beat LeBron, in a way, by becoming him. (And then they kept beating him, and everyone else, by adding Kevin Durant to the roster.) As more and more of the sport's inefficiencies get ironed out with each passing season and as the number of possessions in a given game continues to grow, the advantage of having the best player has steadily diminished. After all, LeBron has been to nine finals, and his teams were favored to win the title just twice. Meanwhile, Jordan's Bulls were favored every time they were there.

For some, Jordan's unblemished finals record will forever be the ultimate proof not just of his supremacy but proof of the idea that if you're *really* the best, you'll always find a way to win. LeBron will never be considered the greatest basketball player of all time by everyone who cares to consider these things. That zero in Michael Jordan's loss column will never budge, while James's six defeats might even grow from there.

James may go down as the greatest loser in history. Only Jerry West has lost more NBA Finals games than LeBron, and it's possible that James finishes his career atop that list. Of course, James has reached more finals than Jordan ever did. To lose so many finals games, you have to get there year after year after year.

Two White Kids from New York Kicking Ass

BRIAN PLATZER

Michael Landers, twenty-four, and Mark Croitoroo, twenty-seven, have been best friends for a long time. At a table tennis tournament nearly a decade ago, an opposing coach went after Michael, calling him *spoiled* or *hot shit* or something like that. The details are murky, but both Michael and Mark recall Mark getting in the grown man's face and threatening him to defend Michael. "You're picking on a fifteen-year-old," Mark yelled. "Let's fight. Right now. You go after Michael, you'll have to come through me first." At the time, Michael and Mark were two of the best young table tennis players in the United States.

MARK WAS VERY GOOD, but Michael was better. As an eleven-year-old at the 2005 Junior Olympics, Michael finished first in under-12 doubles and second in under-12 singles. Three years later, he became one of the youngest Americans ever to win the national singles championship. Table tennis (a name preferred over "ping-pong" by serious competitors, though it's not unusual to hear players say "ping-pong" or even "pong") is a sport that can favor older, more experienced players. Many peak in their twenties or even thirties, but Michael was the country's best player at fifteen years old. At seventeen he was on his way to the Olympics. Publicity followed. NPR dedicated a national segment to him. He was the only table tennis player ever to be on two different cereal boxes. He starred in a widely released documentary.

But, in the Olympic Trials, Michael lost. He didn't make the team.

"I had an off day," he told me with a relaxed smile, years later. "I could have won, but it wasn't my day."

Now, Michael gives lessons at SPIN, the same Manhattan table tennis club where he trained nearly every afternoon in his early- and midteens. He's studying for a master's degree in social work from the University of Buffalo. He wants to help people. When I first met him during a table tennis lesson more than a year ago, he said he was happy. But I didn't believe him. The idea of a celebrated prodigy returning to his old training grounds in order to give lessons to me—a writer with a fledgling backhand—struck me as necessarily tragic. When my first novel didn't sell, I avoided bookstores for months, and here he was forced to be a high-profile failure in the very room where he'd spent years preparing for Olympic glory.

But when we recently met up again—this time at The Bean, a chain coffee shop near the East Village apartment Michael shares with his girlfriend—every time I'd badger him to admit he was miserable, he'd deny it. And then he'd pivot to Mark.

"You must be heartbroken!" I said.

"You should really talk to Mark," Michael responded, smiling again. "I'm happier now than I've ever been, and so is he. Mark had it way rougher than I did. He's doing great now. Why can't you believe that I am too?"

MICHAEL AND MARK REFER to each other as best friends. They're both New Yorkers who dedicated their childhoods to table tennis, and, in their midtwenties, both are trying to figure out what role the sport should play in their adult lives. Just under six feet tall, they're both thin, fit, and lithely muscular. Their bodies bounce when they walk, and their hands are constantly in motion: fidgeting, peeling labels, tearing napkins, stirring drinks. They play a similar, aggressive style that relies on powerful forehands to finish points. They've had many of the same coaches and met with the same psychologist. And although Michael—lighter in features and demeanor—grew up on Long Island, and Mark—intense, neurotic—is a Manhattan kid, they share verbal mannerisms. They both stop midsentence to take deep breaths, which precede a rush of words that seem out of their control.

When I reached out to Mark, he suggested we meet at

Caffe Reggio, a Greenwich Village institution that claims to have served America's first cappuccino. I asked if I could get him a pastry or maybe that famous cappuccino, but he said he only cheats with gluten or dairy twice per week. I told Mark that he and Michael speak in similar ways, and he looked at me like I'd just pointed out that table tennis is played with a ball that bounces on a table. "We spend a lot of time together," he said.

TOP SPIN, the documentary that featured Michael, made it seem as though he was forced to drop out of high school and take online classes in order to focus on table tennis. But in reality Michael was thrilled to have the excuse.

"Around middle school and high school, I got bullied a lot for playing ping-pong. There was nothing physical, but just in general it got to the point where I didn't feel safe. Ping-pong was a great ticket to get the fuck out of there. And my parents were on board too? It was awesome!"

Mark experienced something similar at St. Ann's, the prestigious Brooklyn private school. "Ping-pong was more frowned upon than looked highly on," he said. "You know kids are just being kids. I think a lot of the time people want to fit in so they go toward the norm where they can feel safe. Straying away from the community is scary, so they can't say *that's cool* if their friends don't think it's cool."

Would he have ever gone the online-classes route?

Again, he looked at me like I was an idiot. "My father

wouldn't have let me in a thousand years. He believes in putting yourself in hard situations and making the most of them. And I wouldn't have wanted to." Even though he had dyslexia on top of learning disabilities, he wouldn't drop out. That would be giving up, something Mark doesn't do.

MARK MET MICHAEL AT a tournament when they were both starting out. "Michael seemed like a nice kid," Mark said. "I was fifteen, he was twelve. People knew that Michael would be a good player. His parents were very dedicated to getting him the right help. My parents put the responsibility of finding a coach and living and everything on me, but Michael's parents were very hands-on. I mean, don't get me wrong. My parents paid for everything, took me to tournaments, all that. But Michael's parents were totally involved."

This is typical of the way Mark talks. He tells me he doesn't blame his parents before I thought he was blaming them. He anticipates and confronts conflict.

It wasn't only Michael's parents who gave him a leg up. Michael was beloved in the table tennis world. According to Mark, "It was always about Michael. With my coach. With everyone. There was this entire movie about him! Other players would like him just because he was good. Like him personally. And it was worse than that because people would mistake me for him. Two white kids from New York kicking ass. They'd always see us together. But when they realized I wasn't him, they'd give me shit. A lot of players didn't like me because I was very aggressive. When you're a champion, everyone likes you. A lot of players gave him so much respect. I was the kind of guy who people kind of laughed at."

How bad did it get?

"I slammed a lot of rackets," Mark said. "Threw tables. I got warned before every match almost. I was the bad boy of table tennis. I got a lot of attention from it. Michael got attention for winning, I got attention for my anger."

TABLE TENNIS TOURNAMENT MATCHES are best out of seven games, each game win-by-two up to eleven points. Michael starts close to the table. Serving, he often moves out beyond the far left side of the table, his front leg at the table's back left corner, his back leg a couple feet behind him, farther left. Michael tosses the ball high, but his head stays steady. He stomps his left foot when striking the ball. He keeps the serve low, usually down the middle so his opponent can't extend his arms. When he returns the serve, he stands left but less so, only enough to give his forehand more room to operate. He squats low on his muscular legs, eyes not much higher than his opponent's stomach. Michael gives the impression of a coiled python painfully eager to strike. He thinks three or four shots ahead, bullying the other player into floating something Michael can attack with his looping, overpowering forehand or quick-snap, blink-and-you-miss-it backhand.

Mark plays in a similar style but rarely holds himself back.

He hits hard whenever possible, though Mark's hardest doesn't compare to Michael's.

These guys are geniuses in one very small arena of life, and watching them play is as thrilling as watching James Harden or Roger Federer. A spectator experiences a familiar combination of tension in waiting for the results and awe in what these athletes' bodies can do. Most points last only a few seconds. They are abbreviated chess matches thought out three shots at a time.

Michael's vicious power lies dormant, as he and his opponent lean—in what looks like frustration—over the table, spinning the ball low, so the other player must do the same. Players at Michael's level can hit a ball that spins 150 full rotations per second, but Michael is not a "ball control" player, someone who uses spin, change of pace, and consistency to force mistakes. Michael is an attacker seeking that opportunity to pounce. In the rare case that his opponent manages to return Michael's big forehand, both players retreat two, three, four feet behind the table, knees bent deep, bodies crouching to defend and rising to attack. When given the opportunity to strike, Michael generates power from his legs and a full rotation of his thighs and hips. Michael is like a Major League Baseball player turning on a fastball and instantaneously preparing to hit the next one. Though table tennis balls tend to be hit at just over fifty miles per hour, players have only a few feet to adjust. At this speed, the ball travels the length of table in about an eighth of a second.

Low serve, short return with added spin, another short

return, a blocked or chipped backhand, a controlled forehand with heavy spin, and on and on until one of the two players hits with less spin or higher on the table, at which point the other player attacks and wins the point or trades powerful strokes until one is too much for his opponent to handle.

MICHAEL UNDERSTOOD some aspects of Mark's feelings toward him: "Part of Mark hated me. We had arguments. But he was someone I trusted more than even my family. He was my one best friend. When I would see other people, I would never get *how are you doing*, it was always how great I was. I was the ping-pong guy. Even with my parents. I tended to behave toward my parents in the way in which I thought they viewed me. I did that for a lot of interactions. I didn't want to be vulnerable or show weakness. I needed Mark because he was a real friend I could be honest around."

"I remember a few times trying to stop the friendship," Mark said. "One time in China he made fun of me for not doing well in some drill. He allowed people to make fun of me in a way that I would never allow people to talk about him. I had very high expectations of him—that he would fistfight someone for me—and that was way too demanding. I was looking for reasons to fight people. But he was a very soft guy. A very gentle guy. I don't think I understood that when I was younger. I thought everyone saw him as a champion. *You have everything. What do you have to complain about?* But we were jealous of each other. I was jealous of him because he was the better player. I don't know why he was jealous of me. He always looked up to me. He's told me that. I was his only friend."

Did some part of Mark hate Michael? Resent him, at least? Did Mark root against Michael after he—Mark—was out of the tournaments?

"It wasn't jealousy," Mark said. "I mean, there was some of that. I wish that I could have been happier for myself. I won two titles in the nationals. But only in my divisions. He won the entire nationals. And at times there was part of me that wanted him to lose because if he won I felt he might be a meaner person. There was a part of me that felt that if Michael wins, he'll treat people badly. It wasn't mostly jealousy. It was fearing the way he would act when he won. Of course I wanted him to win, though. More than not. For sure."

THE AMERICAN OLYMPIC TABLE tennis team is combined with that of the Canadians. Together, the United States and Canada only send three male singles players to the Games. The best players from both countries are invited to the Olympic Trials based on their rankings, and three days of matches determine who gets to represent their countries. To make the team in 2012, Michael had to win a single-elimination tournament on the first or second day, or succeed in the round-robin tournament on the third day (round-robin, because day three also determined the alternates for each team) in order to make it to a final single-elimination phase.*

The first day of the 2012 Olympic Trials, Michael lost a heartbreaker to Pierre-Luc Hinse, 11–8, in the seventh, deciding game. It was a great match between two superb players. On the second day, Michael lost again to Hinse, this time more quickly. And on day three, during the round-robin tournament Michael lost to a *different* Canadian named Pierre-Luc—Pierre-Luc Thériault—ensuring Michael would not make the team. Tape of Michael's losses to the two Pierres-Luc suggests that Michael may have been outmaneuvered: lulled by ball controllers into attempting to hit forehand smashes before gaining command of the point.

Or possibly, as Michael says, he just had a couple off days. Had he made fewer unforced errors, he would have looked like a strategic genius or athletic force.

"SO," I SAID TO MICHAEL. "You and Mark were very close friends. You were winning tournaments. Mark was winning matches but struggling to be happy. And then you lost."

* To confuse things further, both the United States and Canada were guaranteed at least one player on the team, and this year, Canada had promised a spot to a recent Chinese immigrant who couldn't attend this tournament due to passport problems. China is better at table tennis than any country is at any other sport. Trials to make the Chinese Olympic team are much more difficult than the Olympics themselves. At the 2016 games, there were 172 table tennis players, and at least 44 were born in China. Only six represented the country, while the rest had found citizenship elsewhere. Over 31 percent of table tennis Olympians were born outside the nation they represented, whereas the next closest sport for foreign nationals, basketball, came in at 15 percent.

"And then I lost," Michael said.

"And you were devastated?" I said.

"No," Michael said. "Why do you keep asking me that? I wasn't devastated."

He dropped the open smile. "What I've always been very good at," Michael said, "is taking feelings from losses and immediately throwing them to the back of my mind. In general, I'm very good at distracting myself. It was a way to cope. After I lost, it would not be in my mind. I learned it from my mom. My entire family for the most part has a self-image that is overwhelmingly positive and happy. I think when you have a self-image that's overwhelmingly positive, it's a little bit easier to push the bad feelings out of there because it'd be going against how you feel you are."

It was the dogged perseverance and an ability to immediately forget mistakes that made Michael so successful, and it was those same characteristics that allowed him *not* to be devastated by falling just short of achieving his dreams. It was exactly the talent to forget a bad point and bounce back to win the next one that lets a champion move on from the type of loss that would have derailed my life.

But when I suggested as much to Michael, he wasn't convinced. "For me, yes. Maybe. But not for everyone. Not for Mark. Mark needs to keep going until he gets it right."

"So you just quit?" I asked.

"Not really. I went to college. I started over. The social stuff was hard again, but I was okay."

AFTER MICHAEL LOST THOSE Olympic Trials, life got better for Mark.

"My head was just more clear," Mark said. "I was getting older. I was starting to become more aware of the intellectual and psychological parts of the game. It was kind of great. No matter what people said about my age or technique, I knew it wasn't true what they were saying. It was for me to decide what I can do and what I can't do. Between nineteen and twenty-two, I started to understand. I left Columbia to go try to make the Olympics."

And this coincidentally happened when Michael stopped training so hard?

"Yeah. I don't know. Maybe not. I think I finally understood that we had a great friendship. Now we could just be friends."

"Because he was no longer training as hard."

"Maybe, sure. And Michael got me into Ochsenhausen—a training center in Germany. The second best in the world. They accepted me as a joke. They don't let Americans in, but Michael vouched for me. He'd played there years before. I arrived and I saw those players playing, and I said, *Those guys are the best guys here, right*? And they said, *No, they're the worst*. It was like magic over there. It was kind of amazing. I was top-sixteen at the time for US citizens. But they almost kicked me out because I couldn't keep the ball on the table. Everything was sped up. Technique, footwork, stance, timing. I was there for two months, and it was like going to school. Everything came together. Every question I ever had to ask about the game was answered. This was three years ago. I finally understood everything I wanted. I had thirty extra pounds of muscle, hitting like a monster for my forehand. I was in training. I finally had all the answers."

So Michael quit and suddenly Mark found all the answers.

"But then I went to Hungary and played a league to prep for Olympic Trials, and I injured my right arm. The forearm of my playing arm wouldn't move. But I kept training. In my mind it didn't matter that my arm didn't work. I got good at making adjustments to completely avoid my backhand. I learned to calm down. But my injury I couldn't solve. My arm was just crippled. After one match, I couldn't even hit my forehand anymore. I went to the locker room and started to cry. I felt very lonely. I was in a very dark place. Losing hair. I was breaking down. I think it was an accumulation of being so pissed off all those years. I overtrained and didn't sleep and would still go play. I was intense, depressed. People were very worried about me. I couldn't play in the Trials, which made me worse. I learned that going to so many different environments could be dangerous to one's mind. I went from Columbia to Germany, California, Hungary, Austria, Germany, and back home right back to Columbia. I was going crazy. My neck was in so much pain. I couldn't sleep at all. And no one knew why. No one could fix me."

"No one?"

"Not until Michael introduced me to his psychologist. He was able to help me. He showed me that I wasn't living in reality. The reality is that I can't play at a world-class level right now. My arm doesn't function like it used to."

"But I thought you still play?" I said.

"Lefty," he said.

"What?"

"I play lefty," he said. "Michael helped me get through the really dark place. I was a beginner, but it's better to hit the ball than not hit it. Michael's been there for me. He's my best friend. Lately, I've been improving, lefty. I'm getting better really quickly. Getting good. And even though we're giving more people citizenship and our juniors are getting better, if I dedicated myself to this, I could do it. Even though I'm doing it for fun and they're doing it to make the Olympics."

"You're not doing it to make the Olympics?" I asked. "From what I can tell, you need to keep going. You can't stop."

"I'm not as emotionally invested in the results, but I'm definitely still crazy about table tennis. And . . . I do have a second arm to be trained. Maybe one day I'll decide I want to do it. Go professional. Play league in Europe. Train for the Olympics. It's possible, if I dedicate everything, I can do it. Lefty. I love table tennis. My body is only getting stronger and more flexible the older I get. I'm finally sleeping. I do a lot of qigong now. My body is only getting younger. I don't know how good I'll get. If I get good enough when I'm forty, I'll go for it then. If I keep playing, I'll get better. Now I don't have a mental limitation. I understand the game better.

I understand myself. I don't lose my temper. If I try hard, put on thirty pounds of muscle, train—yeah, I'd bet on me. I'd bet money on myself."

MICHAEL ENJOYS HITTING WITH Mark three times a week. They chat, catch up on life, on Michael's girlfriend and studies, on Mark's business (a virtual reality theme park in Vegas) and improving left-handed game.

"Amazing," I keep saying as Michael laughs. "And I believe you've gotten over losing in Olympic Trials. But I still can't believe that you're comfortable being back there, giving lessons."

"It's absolutely uncomfortable training people at SPIN," he said. "But not because it was where I trained for the Olympics. There was a time when, teaching someone for the first time, I would take thirty-minute walks before to calm down because I was so nervous about being myself and being okay with anything that happened on the table. I am more down on myself when I can't help someone hit a forehand than when I didn't make the Olympics. What used to happen was that if I would make a suggestion and within the first six and a half seconds it wouldn't be fixed, my mind would start going *fuck, fuck, fuck me.* I'd blame myself. It was about how the other person was perceiving me. One of the reasons why I've kept teaching is because I realized the potential for *leaning into the discomfort* as they say in social work."

"It's the same thing you felt in high school!" I said, laughing.

"Yeah," he said slowly. "Yes. I guess so. I've never thought about it like this. But when you put it like that, it's absolutely true. The pressure I felt going into a lesson was so much more than the pressure I felt at Olympic Trials. But it is the exact same pressure I felt while walking down the hallway in school. I'm using table tennis. I want to grow. I want to be able to transcend the discomfort. You can go to therapy and talk about the experiences you're having, but that doesn't come anywhere close to being able to experience the discomfort in real time while working on yourself. When I'm teaching, I try to be as aware as possible of what's going on within me.

"The table tennis side of it is incidental to where my life is, today. Ping-pong is just the arena where I happen to be able to help myself and other people. It's where I have skills and credentials. It lets me do what I need in order to become a more confident, happier man."

And if you believe him, then that's great. Really great. He's never been happier. Him or Mark.

Too Lucky in Love

JOSHUA PRAGER

Word reached Bobby Thomson that he was wanted outside, that only a curtain call might dissipate the stubborn throng chanting his name. And so, minutes after his home run in the last half-inning of a playoff game had won the 1951 pennant for the New York Giants, out Thomson went, wading through the packed Giants clubhouse to its top outdoor step.

A roar rose at first sight of the great Scot. Men leaning dangerously over a bleacher's metal rail reached for Thomson, outstretched fingertips inches from his thick brown hair. Thousands more reached up from the rectangular patch of grass beneath him, though a touch was impossible. It was a delirious crowd, and Deputy Inspector Cornelius Lyons and his detail of cops struggled to safeguard the green concrete and wooden staircase that led to the afternoon's hero.

Thomson waved and waved. The cheers were deafening, "the most frenzied 'curtain calls,'" wrote John Drebinger in the *New York Times*, "ever accorded a ballplayer." They were anesthetizing too. The home run had left Thomson feeling queasy, but after a dozen or so swells, he ducked back into the clubhouse feeling only alive.

The pitcher who had surrendered Thomson's home run, meantime, felt sick—Brooklyn Dodger Ralph Branca recumbent on a wooden clubhouse step, crying into folded arms.

"Why me?" Branca muttered to himself. "Why me? Why me?" It was a question that the pitcher had posed and answered years before, wondering as to his physical gifts, concluding that they were given him by God to help shoulder the burden of provision for his parents and fourteen siblings. But now he wondered as to his misfortune, and teammate Duke Snider, overhearing Branca as he shuffled by, offered no reply.

Easier for the centerfielder was to bid, next door, his defeater luck, which he now did together with a cast of broken well-wishers—Jackie Robinson, Pee Wee Reese, Preacher Roe, Roy Campanella, Clem Labine. The last offered Thomson a handshake. "Nice going, Bobby," he said. "Good luck in the Series." Thomson did not recognize the crew-cut blond. "I pitched against you yesterday," said Labine. With that, the right-hander left.

Branca lifted himself to his size-13 feet, stepped to a water fountain, bowed, drank, straightened. Nowhere was there refuge. The pitcher meandered, pounding a fist against whatever passed—a concrete wall, a run of wooden lockers—then returned to a step and to sobbing.

It was now, denied entrance some 15 minutes, that the press finally swooped in on Brooklyn's green crypt to scavenge for quotes.

No one spoke to Branca. And Branca, brown eyes cast down, spoke to no one, reporters waiting just feet from the pitcher to catch whatever would be his first words. Minutes passed, five then ten, Branca hearing well with his large ears the thrum of celebrating Giants and their ovations outside. The pitcher stopped crying and spoke. "I guess," he said, a passel of pencils sprung to life, "I'm too lucky in love to be lucky at anything else."

Here was a first stab at understanding. No matter that Branca had long mocked Lady Luck, had walked beneath ladders, worn number 13. Desperation breeds faith, the pitcher in want of a logic to his suffering. And so now he found one. He was to be married in 17 days and Ann Mulvey would still love him.

The AP, though, wanted more, wanted a goat's take on what had transpired afield. And so, though Branca resisted—"Leave me alone," he said. "Just leave me alone."—Will Grimsley, a red-headed reporter from Tennessee, did not, and the pitcher finally succumbed, turning to an 0-1 fastball.

"It wasn't a bad pitch," Branca offered in low voice. "I didn't think he hit it too well. It was sinking when it went in to the stands." Another reporter approached, and the pitcher continued. "I guess we weren't meant to win it," he told Roscoe McGowen of the *New York Times*. "The ball was high and inside, not a good pitch [to hit], and it only cleared the wall by this much." Branca held his large hands inches apart, indicating his margin of loss.

One room away, a horde of press looked to Thomson for *his* take. And in the aftermath of a home run, pitcher and hitter were strangely in step.

"If I was a good hitter I'd have taken that one," yelled Thomson to James Dawson of the *Times*, his voice high as helium and hoarsening. "It was high and inside, the kind they've been getting me out on all season." "Honest," Thomson said, "a better hitter would have let Branca's pitch go by for a ball."

And so it was that Branca and Thomson came together. He who had lost stated he had done his job well. He who had won stated he had done his job poorly.

Branca sat on a three-legged stool, face down as a trio of teammates approached. Pitchers Carl Erskine and Labine, whom fate might have stood in his MacGregor spikes, told Branca that he was a victim of circumstance. And Robinson, he who had once known unspeakable loneliness as the only black player alongside 399 whites, and whom Branca had then befriended, tried to comfort him too. "If it wasn't for you," Robinson told Branca, "we wouldn't even have been here."

On the other side of a brick wall, Thomson undressed. His line drive had turned his gear to gold—his Adirondack bat, 34 ounces of lacquered white ash, and his Wilson shoes, black six-eyeleted leather cleats, to be encased in glass. The hero showered then shaved, given as he did by his drunken teammate Hank Thompson an invigorating kiss on the lips.

He dressed, slipping a dark blazer over a white shirt with a plaid collar, a thin strip of tartan extending to his sternum. And after posing for one last photo—cigar in mouth, arm around a security officer—Thomson stepped out into the night, hopping into a cab with teammate Sal Maglie for the CBS TV studio. For a thousand dollars, he would talk to Perry Como. His family could wait.

Just one man, it seemed, remained at the Polo Grounds, Branca bent forward atop his stool. The pitcher now rose. And uncinching the leather belt about his 38-inch waist, he undressed and walked into a concrete shower, naked but for a silver Saint Christopher about his neck. The pitcher stood under cold water for a long while, "to cool my body down," he says. He then toweled dry, put on a blue suit and tie, and stepped down onto the empty field where just to his left rested perspective, a bronze plaque commemorating Eddie Grant, the Giant killed in the Argonne Forest 33 years before in the First World War.

Branca turned toward right field. Confetti underfoot, he walked past the Giants bullpen, on through an upward-sliding metal gate, beneath the stands and into the parking lot, unable even as he opened the driver's door of his Olds to recall clearly what hours before had happened. Ann sat in the back seat in tears, her father's second cousin Francis Rowley, a Jesuit priest, come to console her. Rowley turned to Branca. "Forget it, Ralph," he said, Roman collar about his neck. "It could have happened to anyone. You did your best."

Branca's mind cleared. He had lost the pennant.

Branca had once been a great pitcher. And, at 25, he remained a good man. He did not cheat, did not smoke, and, save an occasional highball, did not drink. And so, he answered Rowley, a man of the cloth, with a desperate and familiar question. "Yes, Father," he said, "but why did it have to be me? Why me?"

Father Rowley, he whose brother James was head of the US Secret Service, understood what it meant to safeguard a public figure. And head of campus ministries at Fordham University, he did not hesitate with his answer. "The reason God picked you to throw that pitch," he said, "was because He knew that your faith was strong enough to withstand the agonies that would follow. That you would know it was His will and you had done your best and no one could ask more of any man."

Branca listened. Here in a sedan in an empty parking lot in Harlem was an answer that made sense, that jibed with scripture and his world view and his sense of self, an answer elastic enough to accommodate all that was sure to follow. Here was a reply tantamount to reprieve. The home run was a crucible. Fiancée at his side, Branca drove off.

This piece has been adapted from Joshua Prager's The Echoing Green: The Untold Story of Bobby Thomson, Ralph Branca and the Shot Heard Round the World.

If You Can't Beat 'Em

LOUISA HALL

1.

One January morning, almost half a century ago, my mother caught my grandmother crying by the tray of African violets on the sill of the dining room window.

When my grandmother realized that my mother was watching, she wiped her tears and set her jaw.

"If you can't beat 'em," she said, "join 'em."

For years, her husband—by all accounts a difficult man; by some accounts violent and abusive—had disdained and discouraged my grandmother's interests, which included irenic pursuits like reading, writing, and flower arranging.

Despite his derision, she had attempted to persist in these interests through half of her marriage. But finally, in that moment by the dining room window, she decided to set them aside and join my grandfather in the pursuit he had been attempting to master for years: the business of breeding and racing thoroughbred horses.

The next day, using her own money, which she had inherited from her mother and her great-aunt, my grandmother bought a thoroughbred racehorse. That horse won its first race. From there, my grandmother was off. She started a horse-breeding business that became far more successful and ambitious than anything my grandfather ever attempted, a coup that has occasionally led me to reflect that perhaps my grandmother didn't actually mean, "If you can't beat 'em, join 'em." Perhaps what she meant to say was: "If you can't join 'em, beat 'em."

She started her business on the Maryland farm that she had bought for her husband, but eventually she moved her horses to France. There, her business thrived beyond any measure my grandfather had managed. Her horses won several of the biggest thoroughbred races in Europe. She co-owned a horse with the Aga Khan. She co-owned a horse with a Mafioso. In the accounts that were made of her business in the months after her death in 1983, her earnings came out several times what she put into the business, which was far more than her husband had ever earned in all his years of pursuing the business.

2.

When I write up a long account of this story and send it to my mother and her four sisters, my mother sends the draft back the same night. It's heavily redlined, largely for stylistic concerns: I'm famous in my family for my bad grammar. She fixes much of the diction as well. At the end, in purple track notes, she writes: "I love it, I love it, my sweetheart. So proud of you for getting it."

3.

The next morning, I find an email from her sister Ellie: "Well, I don't know who you are sending this essay in to," she concludes, "but it is very personal, and I don't know, Louisa, if it leaves more scars and tears and doubt in a person's mind (body, and soul) than not."

4.

Margy writes to me the following night: "Much of what you suggest is acceptable about (my father) is unfamiliar to me, and some of the facts of his relationship with his family also seem a little off the mark."

The next morning, she follows up: "I appreciate your wanting to tell this story, which certainly lends itself to dramatization. I also appreciate your saying that it is 'not my story to tell'—but, as you tell it, it is not always clear whose story it is. I just want to be clear that a good deal of it is not mine."

The next day, she writes again: "I remain troubled by your story," she says. "Particularly your construct of my mother's approach to her marriage as a contest. For example, her horse business always seemed to me initially an accommodation to my father and later an escape from him, not so much a competition with him—though I have no doubt she had some satisfaction in being able to play in a higher-stakes game by virtue of her money. But when we were growing up, she was abused by him, and allowed her children to be abused by him, and looking back on it I cannot recall anything about it that was competitive in any fair sense of that word."

5.

On the one hand, you could tell the story of my grandmother's decision to pursue racing as a final triumph: after years of failing to assert her own interests, she entered my grandfather's race, and—to her credit—she won it.

"My mom," Ellie says, "did more than double her money in the thoroughbred breeding business. She was valiant beyond words."

But you could also tell the same story as a sad capitulation. Instead of leaving an abusive husband, she stayed. She stayed along with her children and tried to impress him by playing the only game he cared about.

"There is no way," Margy says, "that an abused person can ever 'win' a contest with her abuser except by leaving the situation in some fashion."

6.

In trying to accurately describe the story of my grandmother's business, it's impossible not to include a description of my grandfather. If it hadn't been for him, after all, she wouldn't have lived on a horse farm in Maryland.

My grandmother came from Vermont. She met my grandfather when she was twenty-three and teaching French at a girls' school in Baltimore. He was thirty-two and struggling to build a career for himself. He didn't like working under anyone, but he loved Maryland, and he also loved horses.

Without my grandfather's presence in her life, my grandmother never would have purchased one racehorse, let alone several of the most successful thoroughbreds in Europe.

Left to her own devices, she'd have pursued other interests. In general, the pursuits she chose before she entered the business were contemplative, nonathletic, solitary. She spent hours at her typewriter; she listened to opera alone. According to my mother, when my grandmother heard the sound of the screen door slam, signaling her husband's return from the farm, she shoved the Victrola under the bed.

She did join a flower club, but—according to Dotty, another one of my mother's sisters—when her friends from the club called to make plans for local events, her husband mocked them, and eventually they stopped calling.

It was my grandfather, not her, who loved competition. It was he who, by all accounts, organized his family's life around an endless series of athletic contests.

To some extent, therefore, the way you view my grandmother's decision to enter the horse racing business depends on how you view my grandfather. It also depends on how you understand competition.

7.

My mother, who has always been a fierce competitor—a tennis champion in her childhood, a golf phenomenon in her adulthood—remembers her father's presence at every tennis match she ever played.

She remembers his grin when she challenged him to race home from the barns while evening fell and the swallows swooped low overhead.

She also remembers him setting up a fistfight on the lawn between her sister Dotty and a boy named Carter Crew. After listening to them bickering in the backseat of the car, her father decided they should settle the matter "like men." While Dotty and Carter circled each other—both crying, neither wanting to punch—he urged his daughter to land the first blow. This lasted until his wife, my grandmother, came out of the house and begged her husband to call off the fight.

After that, my mother remembers her father striding over to my grandmother, pushing her through the dining room door, then shoving her into the fireplace, where she hit her head on the mantel. Knocked out, she slid down to the floor and remained there until her husband picked her up and carried her upstairs to the bedroom.

8.

"I don't actually remember that scene with my mother happening on the same day as the Carter Crew fight," my mother writes back, when I show her this passage.

I realize it was Dotty who told me that scene happened on the same day as the fight.

My mother also redlines the rest of the article.

"She remembers his grin *of affection*," she writes.

9.

Later in the day, I get an email from my father, from their house in Wyoming. "Mom shared with me her revisions of your article," he writes. "I think it is wonderful. You have captured a different perspective from the rest of us, which is excellent and even healing."

He has also redlined my mother's redlined piece. He's taken out, for instance, "She remembers his grin of affection."

In his version, the line reads: "She remembers momentary flashes of affection."

10.

My mother says her father was occasionally tyrannical. But she also says that, overall, she remembers him fondly. He was her father. She loved him, and she felt his love for her in exchange.

When I ask her how she felt his love, she tells me that when he challenged her to walk across the highest, narrowest rafter in the barn to collect a nest of chicken eggs, and she did it, and came down alive, clutching two unbroken fistfuls of eggs, she felt the warmth of his pride.

She tells me that, when a neighbor asked her to ride a pony too wild for her to handle in a regional horse show, her father considered his little daughter and said, "Do you really want to do this?" And without pause, my mother said yes, and in the way he looked at her then, she felt how much he admired her courage.

Now, all these years later, she tells me that pride and love aren't so different. Her father, she says, more than her mother, appreciated her ebullient, competitive nature. Her mother, on the other hand, was distant and somewhat aloof, preoccupied with the drama of her own relationship with her husband.

Her father was *there*. So even now, it's difficult for my mother to condemn him.

When I press her, for instance, about his tendencies toward violence, she concedes that he was occasionally overcome by his rage. But she reminds me of his tenderness with animals.

He would have gone to any length, she says, to save a nest of abandoned chicks. He'd carry them, shivering, into the mudroom, where he'd make them a nest of rags in the laundry basket, warm them with a hot light bulb, and kneel beside them on the linoleum floor, feeding them whiskey from an eyedropper.

Even now, she says, she feels his presence. She can still see him perfectly clearly: the way he stood outside the barn with his arm on the gate, gazing over the hills. Six foot four, wearing his Irish wool cap, and a sweatshirt and corduroy pants that had shrunk too much in the laundry. She remembers his exposed wrists, his calloused fingers, his worn leather work boots. She remembers his face, looking across the expanse of his land as though that farm were a kingdom.

11.

One way of telling the story of my grandfather's influence on my grandmother's decision to go into the horse racing business would be to stick to my mother's side of the story.

She's the sister I know best, and she's told me stories of her childhood since I was a little girl. I've always loved to listen to them. Her stories are lyrical and violent and romantic: they involve riding over mist-shrouded hills; breaking furious yearlings; pony shows, betting sheets, whiskey-soaked cockfights. Her stories are amazing. I've always wanted to write them.

But then it's impossible to write my mother's story without involving her four sisters. They're a part of every anecdote. And each of her four sisters has a different view of their father.

12.

After reading her emails, I try to summarize Margy's opinion of her father in a way she'll approve of.

She writes back from a conference she's attending: "How about this as a substitute: 'Margy, the oldest, describes him as a deeply troubled man who acted out his frustrations on his family, creating a climate of fear and secrecy with the constant possibility of violence. "The best I can say of him," she says, "is that I survived him."'"

I venture a few revisions on my section of the quote.

Margy writes back: "Not quite." She gives me another quote.

Trying to be writerly, I change "acted out" to "enacted."

"No, really," she writes, "enacted is incorrect. I meant acted out."

The next day, when she's gotten home from her conference, she writes to me from her apartment in Washington, DC:

"If you want to mention me at all, you can say this: 'Margy, the oldest, describes him as a cruel and violent man who enjoyed making people afraid of him. "The best I can say of him," she says, "is that I survived him."'"

13.

Ellie and Dotty—the twins—were born after Margy, and they also diverge in the ways they depict him.

Ellie defends her father from her sisters' charges. She remembers her father as supportive, if dominating and insistent.

That's Ellie's quote: "supportive, if dominating and insistent."

At first, I'd written "supportive and warm." But when I show her my initial attempt at describing her perspective, she promptly responds from Munich, where she lives, with an email entitled "Some Important Changes."

Ellie is an artist. She is specific about the wording she wants me to use. "Louisa . . ." she writes, "after supportive put demanding and mean, tyrannical and cruel even. But he had a warmth in him, by contrast, and he was humorous and tender, especially in his apologies to my mother."

Later, she changes this to "supportive, if dominating and insistent."

She sends me other revisions, as well, and several new anecdotes to include about traveling with her father. "DO YOUR BEST TO MAKE THESE FEW IMPORTANT CHANGES TO SHARPEN IT," she says.

14.

Like my mother, Ellie recalls that her father loved animals. She remembers traveling with him to the sales grounds at Deauville. She remembers standing beside him, watching the young horses galloping on the downs at Newmarket. She says that on those trips he had a comfortable, fatherly way. She remembers his humorous opinions of people, his talent for turning a phrase. She concedes that he could be mean, even cruel, but she thinks his toughness taught his girls perseverance and an aversion to injustice.

"He was a man," Ellie says, "who was a bully, but who hated a bully, and who had a strangely contrasting sense of pity for innocent things in danger."

Then she reminds me that he "clobbered Roland McKenzie at a cocktail party" after Roland McKenzie insulted my grandmother.

"He was a defiant, proud SOB," Ellie says. "Daddy, I am winking at you because you know how I mean this!"

15.

In another email, Ellie takes a more subdued tone. Of her mother, she says:

"I just wish she had never met my father, but that is fate and that is kismet and that is life, full of sorrow. Full of the downside. We can only forgive ourselves in order to survive. One can only counteract it with beauty, physical beauty, and the beauty of grace."

She signs off: "A lot of fierce hugs to you. I love you. Ellie."

16.

It's late at night in Munich when Ellie she sends me her final round of revisions. She follows this with one last email.

"Right-o, Louisa. It was a lot of fun for me to work with you like this. Brings me closer to you! And you all, my family there. Here it is a little lonely just now."

17.

Dotty, Ellie's twin, doesn't defend her father at all.

Dotty sits with me on the porch of her house in Montana, under a shivering aspen, and tells me she can still feel the horror involved in circling Carter Crew, knowing that if she didn't punch, someone else would be made to. And she remembers other incidents, too, like when her father dragged her mother down the hall into the bedroom while she cried and begged him to stop.

Dotty calls her father abusive. She finds it appalling that her mother—who had five girls to look after, who proudly called herself a feminist, who had money of her own, and a master's degree in French literature, and read books by Henry James and taught her daughters to always keep their bank accounts separate from their husbands' money—didn't leave the bully she'd married, allowing her girls to grow up in a house in which the consequences of having less physical strength than a man were made all too apparent.

When I ask Dotty if she wants to make notes on my description of her relationship to her father, she says, "It's your story, Louisa. You tell it the way that you want to."

18.

My mother was born after the twins, followed four years later by Molly. Molly is quiet and gentle by nature, and steers clear of words like *abuse.* Like my mother and Ellie, she also remembers her father's warmth: the way he'd pick her up, hold her close, and ask whom she loved best, him or her mother.

But she also remembers the night when, at dinner, her father threw a pewter trivet at her mother's head. Just in time, her mother protected her face by raising her hand and blocking the trivet. After dinner, Molly helped bandage her mother's cut and bleeding fingers. Later that night, her mother left. Molly remembers sitting at the hall window, watching the taillights of her mother's car recede down the long driveway, and feeling overwhelmingly lonely.

19.

When I show Molly this description, she responds from her house, which is down the road from Dotty's house in Montana: "One more thought, just for you, not to be included unless you want. Though there were tender moments with me indeed, as I look back, it's not those moments that stand out so much. Daddy's drive to dominate and control everything around him made him push everything beyond its reasonable limit, often to failure. While he might have shown some inhibition with his children and with Mom, he was often mercilessly physically cruel to the animals if they didn't behave as he wanted them to."

20.

When I show my mother what I've written so far, she writes back from Wyoming. "That's *my* story. It was *me* who was sitting by the hall window, watching my mother leave."

Then she concedes that it's possible that they both sat by the hall window, watching their mother leave.

Like Molly, she remembers the red taillights receding in the fading light of the evening. She also remembers, later, in the darkness of night, feeling somehow both relieved and disappointed when she saw the pale beams of her mother's headlights, turning back in.

Wobbling down the dark, uneven slope of the driveway. Coming to a stop in front of the kitchen door, then blinking out, the car engulfed in new darkness.

21.

"If I may," Margy writes to me from DC, "just as a writer you may want to think about how you reconcile the different parts of your Rashomon story."

I look at the story again. I'm not sure that I can reconcile the parts. Also, I'm not really sure that I want to.

Despite having grown up with a father who treated her unforgivably, Margy became a defense lawyer. She is a former US pardons attorney. At the moment, she's busy making appearances and giving quotes on the history of the presidential pardons. She writes about the crippling lifelong effects of criminal records. She is an advocate for executive clemency, the only constitutional option for clearing a criminal record. She has devoted her life to finding a way for our justice system to extend its most comprehensive mode of forgiveness.

Her sisters have taken different paths, but they've all dedicated themselves with the same passion to caring for beings more vulnerable than they are. My mother worked as a teacher and counselor for high school students. Molly cares for injured animals. Dotty has devoted herself to environmental conservation.

It seems to me that part of the way they were able to emerge from the difficulties of their childhood and maintain such fierce and tender devotions was by learning different strategies for coping with the tensions that filled their family home.

Those strategies colored and shaped what they noticed then, and what they now remember. Gathered together, their impressions of their childhood form a kaleidoscopic picture, the edges blending into each other.

It's interesting, in a literary sense: in terms of building character. But in real life I imagine it's hard for each of them to read their sisters' versions.

22.

From the airport, on her way to Geneva, then Chamonix, where she intends to climb Mont Blanc, Margy writes: "If I had known of (this story) earlier, I might have encouraged you to take a more fictionalized approach, especially in light of the wildly divergent views of my father's character and behavior held by his five daughters, and the inevitable resulting sensitivities."

She has a point. I am a novelist, after all. Perhaps it would have been more discreet to cover this story with a fictional veil.

In previous emails, Margy has mentioned the novel my great-aunt Nancy wrote, a thinly disguised fictional account of my grandparents' life. Great-Aunt Nancy has my grandfather die in an unexpected pitchfork attack.

Margy seems to think this might be a better approach to telling this story than my own increasingly fragmented attempt. But concealing memoir behind a thin layer of fiction has always seemed to me like a slightly patronizing approach, both to the subjects of the memoir and to its readers. Why change the names, when what you really mean, and what everyone knows you really mean, is that you wish the man who assaulted your sister would die in an even more brutal assault?

Fiction, for me, isn't a place to write family stories. For me, fiction isn't a place to write about other people at all. My fiction is the one place where I feel no responsibility to represent other people's perspectives. It's the one place, instead, where in the shelter of my characters' voices, I allow myself to creep toward my own.

23.

But maybe that's what Margy is saying: Write your own version of this story. Don't run around stealing ours.

My grandmother died when I was a baby, so I never knew her. I did know my grandfather when I was a child. We visited him a few times on the farm, and I liked him.

He let me ride the old horses while he led them with a frayed rope. He showed me how to carry warm milk to the barn cats. He taught me how to pick Concord grapes from the vine, and how to eat them by spitting the skins through the gap in my front teeth.

I also remember hiding from him in the barn, squeezed between hay bales, alone in the darkness that was swimming with dust motes. I'm not sure what I'd done, but I remember thinking that if he found me, he'd be terribly angry. I remember the sound of the barn door sliding open, and his shadow looming into the new slice of sunlight.

Even on good days, I sensed in him the potential for fury. Then, a part of me thrilled to that challenge. Once, in the garden behind the house, I turned the hose on him, soaking him through. After an awful, tremulous moment, in which we both hovered on the edge of his potential reactions, he started laughing so hard that he doubled over, clutching his stomach as though I'd actually shot him.

24.

I was probably eight when I formed those impressions of my grandfather. Back then, I hadn't heard the stories my mothers' sisters tell.

Now that I've heard them, I think of him differently. Now nothing in me thrills to the recollection of his fury.

Now I think his behavior was inexcusable. I think he was abusive, and his daughters shouldn't have had to grow up in that house. They shouldn't have had to survive him.

25.

Because this is a true story, or a story I'm trying to make as true as I can, it seems to me that other people's perspectives must be included, at least if I'm aiming for a comprehensive account.

In fact, if that's what I'm aiming for, this story should probably reach beyond even my mother's and my aunts' perspectives. It should also consider, for instance, biographical details that in some way explain—if not excuse—my grandfather's troubled behavior.

His father, for instance, died suddenly when my grandfather was four. He grew up in the Great Depression, sometimes surviving on rice, depending on the generosity of relatives. By the time he was in college on an athletic scholarship, he was already prone to fits of rage. Later, as a newlywed, he enlisted in the Marine Corps after the attack on Pearl Harbor.

His unit was the first to land on Guam. As an engineer, he was among the first men on the beach, establishing supply lines under aggressive artillery fire. During the ensuing battles, his division suffered heavy casualties. Afterward, he was reassigned to an administrative position, but he falsified documents to get himself transferred back to the front lines. The unit where he ended up was one of the first to land on Iwo Jima. He was lucky to survive, but when he came home to his family, his flashes of anger were intensified.

26.

In addition to a longer biographical approach, there is also a broader sociological context.

It should be acknowledged, for instance, that the violence that filled my grandparents' house was an extension of the violence that was rooted in the valley where they chose to live.

After my grandfather returned from the war, he and my grandmother used money she had inherited to buy a farm in Maryland's Western Run Valley, where, before his family's fall from financial grace, his family had owned a plantation.

That valley may have been a beautiful place—as the years passed, their daughters rode horseback through sun-dappled woods, across rushing streams, up grassy slopes—but, of course, it was as brutal as it was beautiful.

Even if no one in my mother's house talked about the slaves who had been tortured and killed there, the slaves whose unpaid work had produced the means for my grandfather's relatives to support him through his genteelly impoverished childhood, the legacy of that violence persisted. It spread into every aspect of life.

People of color in the valley lived in an isolated cluster of houses called Cuba Village, with no electricity or running water. And my grandparents attended the costume ball where Billy Zanzinger killed Hattie Carroll by striking her with his cane when she wasn't fast enough with his whiskey. (Bob Dylan later wrote a song about it.)

Later in the same night, according to articles in the local paper, Billy Zanzinger started beating his wife with his shoe, as though to cleverly demonstrate to the crowd that one form of violence can only lead to another.

A few years after that, my grandparents' neighbor up the hill killed his wife by tying her to a tree outside their house and beating her to death. The police investigators pulled strands of her hair from the tree bark.

In response to such incidents, no one talked my mother or her sisters about racism or sexism, hate crimes or domestic abuse, or any of the other forms of violence that manifested around them. They read glancing mentions in the newspapers. They heard whispers at school, didn't quite understand, and spent their weekends on the backs of unbroken horses, or watching roosters—sharpened spurs attached to their heels—fight to the death in neighborhood cockfights.

27.

And then, of course, there was the racing itself. For the most part, everyone in that valley made a living (or frittered away an inheritance) breeding and training thoroughbred horses to such a fine point of speed and sensitivity that they occasionally killed themselves running. Whipped into competitive frenzy, some horses burst their hearts, racing to win for their owners.

28.

My mother says this description of racing is overkill. She tells me there's beauty in racing. She recognizes the potential for violence, but she reminds me it's the "Sport of Kings." She says that some owners and trainers are cruel, but many are kind. She says horses were meant to run, that they love the people who train them, and that outside the track, they have good lives on the rolling green hills of the farms where they ready themselves for their racing careers.

Dotty agrees, but she reminds me that all too often the relationship between owner and horse veers into domination and cruelty, exploitation of the animal, or even abuse.

As a child, she saw it happen. She remembers the excessive force her father used with the horses. She remembers him subjecting the family dogs to physical tests, like prodding them to cross raging streams they often only barely survived.

Molly remembers him making her help while he choked a cat to death, trying to give it a pill. Even now, she says, she can feel that cat, wrapped in a burlap sack, a living, then dead, weight in her arms.

29.

The next night, from Geneva, Margy writes me an email:

"It is always difficult to try to tell a story from a number of different perspectives. Maybe the problem is that you are trying to tell two stories—one about my father as seen very differently through his several daughters' eyes, and the other about my mother's struggle to maintain her identity with whatever means she had at hand (money and good business sense). Maybe you need to decide which is your main story and sacrifice some of the other. If it were me, I'd be inclined to focus on the marriage 'contest' as it played out in my mother's business interests, which has the added virtue of providing some very interesting details about a world many know little or nothing about. Just a thought. Good luck! Margy."

30.

She's right. I've strayed much too far from my grandmother's story. In my defense, however, that's always been the case in stories about my grandmother: whenever my mother's sisters talk about her, they tend to slip back into talking about their father.

Like all bullies, he takes up more than his fair share of the print. His tendency toward domination persists in the stories his children tell, and the story I'm telling. Maybe, then, it's time to give my grandmother her due.

My grandmother, it should be acknowledged, was lucky. That she was able to enter the business at all was a privilege afforded by her inherited wealth. She was fortunate, as well, in her first horse, which won its first race.

But she deserves credit too. She proved herself to be a canny investor. She scrupulously researched the horses she purchased, and her instincts were impeccable. With the money she earned from her early wins, she bought a single breeding share of Jim French, a small, drab horse who went on to place second in the Kentucky Derby and the Belmont Stakes, and third in the Preakness.

The rest of Jim French's shares, it turned out, were owned by Robert LiButti, the mobster with ties to John Gotti (and, more recently, Donald Trump). When that was discovered, Jim French was impounded. Because LiButti had been banned from racing for life, he was then forced to sell his shares for a million dollars to Daniel Wildenstein, a famous art dealer in Paris. Wildenstein called my grandmother and asked her if she wanted to sell her breeding share, since he was planning to move Jim French to France.

As it turned out, my grandmother did not. Though, in her prim way, she had been horrified to have conducted business with mobsters, she loved Jim French, and cared more about her investment in a good horse than she cared about the rectitude of its former owners.

In fact, after Wildenstein's call, she decided to move *all* her horses across the Atlantic. She'd come to realize that they weren't safe on the farm in Maryland, alongside her husband's horses, when my grandfather allowed a savage horse into the pasture with her best filly.

31.

Dotty tells me that another part of the reason her mother wanted to move her horses away from the Maryland farm is that, as long as the horses were there, they'd never be considered her horses; people would always think they belonged to her husband.

Furthermore, Dotty tells me, she wanted to move her horses to a place where her husband didn't speak the language. When her horses were at home, if people called to talk to my grandmother about them, he sometimes picked up. Inevitably, sometimes disastrously, he meddled in her business operations, as he had with her friends from the flower club. Part of the reason she moved her horses to France, Dotty says, is that my grandfather couldn't speak French, and she could.

So when Daniel Wildenstein called, she kept her share of Jim French and shipped the rest of her horses to Europe, putting an ocean between them and her husband. Once a year, she left the farm in Maryland and traveled to France to stay in a fancy hotel, tend to her business, and watch the races.

32.

This is the part of my grandmother's career to which Margy is referring when she talks about an escape. My grandmother loved going France. She loved the fashion; she loved the food. She loved the people she met there.

She also kept up her winning streak. Later, she bought a half-share of the famous Shergar, a stallion majority-owned by the Aga Khan. Shergar went on to become one of the most successful racehorses in history. He won the Epsom Derby by ten lengths, still the longest winning margin in the race's history.

Her best horse, however, was a mare called Dunette. My grandmother was the sole owner when Dunette won the Prix de Diane, the biggest race in France for three-year-old fillies. The next year, Dunette finished the Prix de St. Cloud in a dead heat with Three Troikas, another horse owned by the Aga Khan. My grandmother—represented by Ellie—won the coin toss to determine who would take home the trophy.

33.

And that's one possible ending for the story of my grandmother's improbable business: with her holding that trophy aloft.

Having escaped to France. Having made a success of the life she made for herself across the Atlantic, if not the life she lived with her husband on the farm they bought in the Western Run Valley.

But there are also other ways of telling the story of her success on the racetrack that complicate such a successful conclusion. Alongside her victories, for instance, there was also a series of devastating reversals. In England, for instance, my grandmother's agent mismanaged her stables and failed to run her horses in several key races. And near the end of my grandmother's life, she chose to bring Dunette back to the United States. In the days leading up to the Washington DC International, a race that was meant to be Dunette's crowning glory—a glory, it should be said, on my grandfather's home turf—Dunette broke her ankle. The injury was so severe that she was nearly put down.

Dunette recovered, but my grandmother blamed herself for pushing Dunette to run that last race. She blamed herself for inflicting on Dunette that long and arduous journey across the Atlantic.

When Dunette retired as a broodmare, my grandmother was offered a million dollars to sell her, but for reasons that may have had to do with her guilt, she chose not to sell. She banked, instead, on the opportunity to make money off Dunette's foals, but for the first three years of Dunette's breeding career, she remained barren. With each year that passed, her market value approached zero, and my grandmother lost additional money attempting to breed her.

The final blow to my grandmother's business came in 1983. At sixty-five, she was dying of breast cancer. In February she received news that Shergar had been stolen from his stable in County Kildare by a gang of masked gunmen. The thieves contacted the Aga Khan to demand ransom, not realizing the stallion had a number of owners. My grandmother, the Aga Khan, and the rest of Shergar's shareholders convened and—not wanting to encourage other thefts of famous horses, and not knowing, in any case, if Shergar had survived the violence of his abduction—decided not to pay the ransom.

By then, my grandmother was terribly sick. She'd lost her hair. She'd grown painfully thin. She'd been told she would die in a matter of months.

It must have been awful for her, at the same time, to be waiting for news of Shergar's fate. When two days passed and the gunmen remained at large, the general assumption was that the horse had been killed. Stallions of that caliber are neurotic and hard to handle. They injure themselves easily. Their injuries are often fatal.

But the search for Shergar continued. A media circus gathered in County Kildare. The investigation was bungled. Jim "Spud" Murphy—the chief superintendent of the Garda in County Kildare—called in an array of clairvoyants, diviners, and psychics. Shergar's body was never recovered.

No charges were ever produced, but the strongest theory to emerge was that the IRA's special operations unit had taken Shergar under the faulty assumption that kidnapping a horse would raise less public outcry than abducting a person.

Years later, the IRA informant Sean O'Callaghan claimed that Shergar had been killed within hours of his theft. According to O'Callaghan, when the horse panicked, so did the thieves. The horse broke his leg, and then the thieves shot him.

Later, another former IRA member told the *Sunday Telegraph*: "Shergar was machine gunned to death. There was blood everywhere and the horse even slipped in his own blood. There was lots of cussin' and swearin' because the horse wouldn't die. It was a very bloody death."

While most of Shergar's owners had insured their shares in the horse, in the days after the theft my grandmother realized that, distracted by her illness, she had forgotten to renew her insurance. So when Shergar wasn't recovered, she lost the small fortune she had invested.

34.

According to my mother, in the last weeks of my grandmother's life, she ran a final inventory of the business she'd started the day after my mother caught her crying by the violets. At that point, Shergar was lost. Dunette was still barren. And when my grandmother finished the math, she was forced to accept the conclusion that her business had lost money overall, though it was close to coming out even.

Weeks later, she died.

If, as I had it in the first draft of this story, some part of her went into the horse business to beat my grandfather at his own game, then she died believing she hadn't. It's somewhat painful to know that, a few weeks after that, Dunette was found to be in foal.

Shortly after that, my mother and her sisters learned that the mare to whom my grandmother had bred Shergar in his first and only year at stud was also in foal.

In the wake of my grandmother's death, when Dunette and her foal and Shergar's filly were sold, my grandmother's business came out at least a million dollars ahead.

35.

In the morning, I find another email from Margy in Geneva. "I think," she says, "when children are encouraged to compete for parental approval, it creates a toxic environment that can do lasting damage.

"Think of this: after my mother died, my father gathered us around the kitchen table and pronounced your mother 'the winner.' And Molly was 'runner-up.' I had no idea (though surely I should have) and was devastated."

Later, she writes again: "Competition is fine . . . what's bad is competing for parents."

36.

That "for" is an unusual conjunction in this context. Usually, after "competing" or "competition," you see the conjunction "with."

"For" is helpful. Maybe the problem with my initial draft was another one of my famous grammar gaffes. Maybe my original mistake was the implication that my grandmother was competing *with* my grandfather.

Maybe the better way of saying it would be to say that she was competing *for* my grandfather.

That she was running to win for her husband.

Dotty tells me that my grandmother tried to be the apple of my grandfather's eye. That was a mistake, Dotty says. In fact he just owned her.

37.

If I imagine it this way, I wish my grandmother had never entered that brutal game. I wish she'd just taken her children and left.

38.

Then I think of Molly at the hall window, watching the taillights of her mother's car, overcome by loneliness.

And my mother, feeling that thud of disappointment

when she watched her mother's headlights bob back down the long driveway.

39.

When I send this to my mother, she writes back, "heartbeat, not thud."

She's right. Heartbeat is definitely better.

40.

I'm amazed at how many times my mother has been willing to read through this piece. But then again, she's always wanted to get this story right. For as long as I can remember, she's been telling and retelling it. She's determined to find the right words to describe the parents she grew up with.

Her sisters are the same. They're real storytellers. They're devoted to detail. And they're determined. They never stop trying to get the damn story straight.

41.

The next afternoon, a few hours after I send her another draft of the piece, Margy writes back.

It's midnight in the little town outside Chamonix, in the shadow of Mont Blanc. She has more notes, and she still doesn't think the different parts of the piece are holding together. She recommends that, instead of trying to reconcile so many different perspectives, I simply tell the story in my own voice. But she ends on a note of encouragement:

"Anyway, you are a talented writer who may in time wrestle this story into some form that will make sense to a larger audience in a larger scheme, even if it is a story that you create yourself. I'm just not sure you have done it here. I'm happy for you to stay in touch.

Love,

Margy."

42.

My mother still plays sports with the same determination she's employed in revising this story. She used to play tennis; now she plays golf almost every day. She only started a few years ago, and already she's a handicap 14.

She says that she likes to compete, but there are bad days when she wishes she didn't. On bad days, she feels her heart in her throat when she lines up to hit a drive. Leaning over a putt, she feels actual terror: as if her whole worth—the value of her entire life—rests on whether she hits the shot right.

On good days, however, when she lifts her club and walks out onto the green, she has a handle on everything that frightens her. Then she plays for the love of the game. Then, despite everything that was terrifying about the way she grew up, she throws her weight into her shots.

She lofts them into the sky. She plays for the power and the speed and the pure undiluted pleasure of winning.

43.

Maybe it was the same for my grandmother. Maybe, on bad days, she watched her horses run with her heart in her throat, imagining that this was her final chance to prove her worth to her husband.

But maybe there were also days when she'd gotten a handle on everything that frightened her. Maybe, then, despite everything that was terrifying about her life with her husband, she leaned on the rail of the track and watched her horses run and felt their power and their speed in her own body.

It's probably true that the only real victory would have been leaving. But still. What a feat.

She was valiant, Ellie says.

Breathtakingly brave.

The champion that her husband wasn't.

44.

After I send this to my mother, she sends it back redlined. She also sends me a text. "Wonderful, wonderful!" she says. "I'm laughing, crying!"

45.

Just before I go to sleep, she sends me another:

"I thought of a new theme for your story. Call me in the morning so we can discuss it!"

The Great Wimbledon FC Heist

RYAN BAILEY

For the outside observer, one of the most puzzling facets of professional American sports is the tendency of teams to relocate. The Utah Jazz, it turns out, do not derive their name from Salt Lake City's rich cultural heritage of African American music. And it is strange for a non-American to see that the good folks of Baltimore were only appeased by the overnight disappearance of the Colts by the arrival of the Cleveland Browns . . . twelve years later. It is accepted that American sports teams are beholden to the whims of their owners and can be moved around the country, with scant regard for the empty-handed fans they leave behind.

Such a culture of sports franchising and transplantation generally does not exist in other parts of the world—perhaps because the concept of ownership is viewed quite differently. In Europe, a soccer team is perceived to be owned as much by the fans and the community as the person who cuts the checks. This is particularly true in the German Bundesliga, where a "50+1 rule" stipulates that all clubs must be majority owned by fans. The community fans that watch and nourish the team are *literally* deemed more important than a majority shareholder. Thanks to this mentality, the European soccer team owner will never be celebrated and thanked on the field after a championship game like they would during the hysteria of a Super Bowl victory.

The biggest European soccer teams may now be owned by Russian oligarchs, Emirati petrodollars, and the same American billionaires who transplant their domestic teams, but they wouldn't entertain the idea of ripping a team away from its home. Manchester City owner Sheikh Mansour is probably aware that he could make more money if his team were based in London—or even his homeland of Abu Dhabi—but he wouldn't dream of moving a club with roots that have been growing in Manchester for over 130 years.

In the United Kingdom, where soccer forms a large part of the national identity and heritage is considered sacred, there has only ever been one example of a team being franchised and ripped away from its fan base.

And it happened to my team.

Back in the black-and-white days of 1889, the students of the Old Central School in the southwest London district of Wimbledon formed a soccer team. They played on the green expanse of Wimbledon Common, around half a mile from the All England Croquet and Lawn Tennis Club, where the first lawn tennis championships had been staged twelve years earlier. Racket sports may have given the area more international acclaim, but the soccer team slowly grew, before Wimbledon FC moved to a nearby disused swampland that evolved into their stadium: Plough Lane.

Operating in very close proximity to bigger teams like Chelsea and Fulham (and in a metropolis with dozens of other teams), Wimbledon attracted a small but devoted fan base. Over the years, the team developed a reputation for outkicking their coverage; they were the scrappy underdog that no one wanted to face on a cold winter afternoon.

During the 1980s, the team rose from amateur obscurity to the top division in the country (before it was known as the Premier League), where they continually put the sword to established teams with significantly higher budgets. The greatest giant-killing feat occurred in 1988, where they defeated Liverpool in the FA Cup final at Wembley Stadium. A frugally assembled team that trained in a public park and spent the evening before the biggest game of their lives drinking in a pub (the same pub on Wimbledon Common where the original nineteenth-century team would get changed before games) beat the biggest team on the planet. Until Leicester City won the Premier League in 2016, it was typically viewed as the most surprising result in the sport.

My father, a fan of his local side since boyhood, started taking my brother and me to Wimbledon games at the point when we were deemed old enough to witness the cursing and ill behavior that were typical of the terraces in the British game. I vividly remember my first match, a 2–1 victory against the aforementioned Leicester in September 1994. The smell of the creaky wooden seats; the older men in sheepskin coats placing bets on the outcome in the stadium bar; the glossy matchday souvenir program, which featured future Hollywood star and Wimbledon "hardman" midfielder Vinnie Jones on the cover.

The team were affectionately known as the "Crazy Gang," due to the overtly physical antics of Jones and the manner in which they gained the edge on more celebrated opposition through psychology and intimidation.

Wimbledon's uncanny ability to play on the same field as the Manchester Uniteds and Liverpools of the world made us everyone's second-favorite team. In sports, there's nothing quite like the inexorable rise of the underdog. But while it could compete on the field, it couldn't compete off it.

Wimbledon were forced to leave their Plough Lane home when it was unable to meet new regulations that required all top division teams to have all-seater stadiums. Plans for a twenty-thousand-seater stadium on a nearby site never materialized, and we were forced to temporarily move in with nearby Crystal Palace at their Selhurst Park stadium.

In his desperation to find a home for the club, Wimbledon's eccentric Lebanese owner Sam Hammam explored some radical solutions, including moves to Cardiff and Dublin. These wild suggestions were pooh-poohed by fans and the English Football Association, who would not entertain the notion of moving a club from its home, let alone to a different country.

In 1997, the club was sold to a pair of successful Norwegian businessman, Kjell Inge Røkke and Bjørn Rune Gjelsten, who had tried and failed to buy Chelsea before settling on the smaller team a few miles down the street. The Norwegians had cultivated their hometown team, Molde, with great success, but their intentions to guide Wimbledon back to their spiritual home proved to be insincere.

In August 2001, the club announced its plan to leave London to move to the town of Milton Keynes, some fifty-six miles north. The threat of a move had been wielded over us before, but this one felt more tangible. We knew we would fight it, but the announcement felt like a swift punch in the gut.

Founded in 1967—making it a baby in comparison to most UK towns—Milton Keynes boasted all the infrastructure and amenities of a modern conurbation, but lacked the one thing that most other urban environments in the UK boasted: a professional soccer team. Rather than invest in and cultivate an amateur team of their own, a Milton Keynes business consortium intended to poach a premade package. In the 1980s, they came close to stealing away Luton Town and also discussed the possibility of stealing London clubs Barnet, Crystal Palace, and Queens Park Rangers. But Wimbledon, with a relatively small fan base, few financial means, and no home of its own, was a perfect target.

Wimbledon fans and their sympathetic rivals vehemently opposed the idea, as did the English Football League, the English Football Association, and even a 150-man Parliamentary Committee. Yes, this issue went all the way to the Houses of Parliament.

Attending games while this controversy raged was a miserable experience. What was once a joyous afternoon with my father and brother turned into a bitter and futile exercise in protest. For the duration of most games, a bilious atmosphere engulfed Selhurst Park as profane chants were directed at the owners. Protest banners that read "A club is for life, not just for profit" and "MK No Way!" were unfurled and the hateful resonance in the air didn't exactly provide the encouragement the team needed. Going to watch the team we loved wasn't fun anymore.

After months of hostility and gut-wrenching protests that carried a feeling of inevitability, the sucker punch came.

In May 2002, after multiple legal battles between the club, the fans, and the soccer authorities, the decision was ultimately handed to a three-person independent arbitration panel. Even at that point, no one in soccer *really* thought we would lose our case. But against all expectation, the panel voted 2 to 1 in favor of the move. With the promise of a lucrative stadium, hotel, and shopping complex, my team had been lured away from the people who created it and rebranded as the Milton Keynes Dons.

My father had attended games since the 1960s and witnessed plenty of defeats in his time, but he had never suffered a loss quite like this. I felt pained by the situation, but he was truly devastated. He didn't burn his jerseys or chain himself to the stadium gates; he simply refused to talk about it and completely lost his vigor. He retreated further into himself. It was heartbreaking.

Our team—the focal point of our community—had been moved away for the sake of a commercial property deal. For weeks, the nauseous feeling at the pit of my stomach was akin to that split second when you feel like you may slip off a tall ladder. The idea of following the team north and watching them have their name, colors, and badge changed was unconscionable.

It was a dark time. For a while, I fell out of love with sports entirely. But rather than wallowing in our collective misery, Wimbledon fans quickly converted the heartache into action. Before long, a phoenix rose from the ashes.

In the immediate aftermath of the decision, a group of Wimbledon fans met at the Fox & Grapes pub on Wimbledon Common—yes, that same location where the original schoolboy team would get changed, and where the 1988 heroes pregamed the FA Cup final. With no right of appeal, the fans in the pub that night agreed that the only course of action was to start a brand-new club from scratch. Exactly two days after the announcement, the Wimbledon Independent Supporters Association held a formal meeting where they agreed to start from scratch again.

And just like that, AFC Wimbledon was born.

The team and league place may have been sold off to the highest bidder, but the soul of this team would remain in place; resurrected through the power of its community. We were turning a loss into a big win.

Fund-raising began immediately. A modest stadium site was located, a new jersey and badge were designed, and public tryouts were held for new players in a park (over 230 plucky amateurs of varying quality showed up). A trust was set up with covenants stipulating that 75 percent ownership of the team would *always* belong to the fans. My father, brother, and I became part owners of the brand-new team and were issued shares that we would never sell and that would never offer a dividend.

All this laborious and bureaucratic work was done in a matter of weeks, by volunteer fans with no experience of league administration, sponsorship deals, or scouting for talent.

But we held a belief in the powerful community spirit that sports can summon.

We knew that fans working to build something they could call their own would be far more rewarding than following a Premier League team with more concern for its stock price than the proletariat who dutifully buy their overpriced tickets and merch. We had witnessed a tiny team rise from the very bottom to the very top against all the odds, and we believed we could make it happen again.

And you know what? It bloody did.

AFC Wimbledon played their first match in 2002. It was a 4–0 loss for a team of players wearing borrowed uniforms who barely knew one another's names. But it was the start of something very special.

The team started out in the amateur ninth tier of the soccer league pyramid and took an unprecedented nine seasons to earn five promotions to reach the professional Football League. AFC Wimbledon had climbed from the very bottom to pro status on a tiny budget—just like the original incarnation had done.

To put the icing on the cake, the ailing Milton Keynes Dons were relegated to the fourth tier in 2018, while the phoenix club that started in protest of their existence played in the league above them.

In September 2015, my father watched in delight as the new iteration of his favorite team came back from 1–0 down to beat Notts County 2–1. The winning goal came with seconds to spare in the ninetieth minute, courtesy of striker Adebayo Akinfenwa, a larger-than-life personality who is well known in the game for his abnormally large frame and power. In the FIFA video game series, he is listed as the strongest player in the world. His heft may affect his pace, but few defenders in the world would relish the prospect of trying to win a 50/50 ball from him. He is as loved as he is feared.

Shortly after the game, no doubt in a jubilant mood from the clutch nature of the win, my father sent me an email to confirm our plan to attend the next home game as a family, along with my brother, just as we had done throughout our youth. Tinged with the same excitement I would feel getting into the back of his sedan to ride to the stadium as a boy, I hit reply. "I'm looking forward to it!" was the cheerful sign-off.

My father never received the reply.

We are given comfort by the fact that one of the last things he did on this earth was to see his team win in emphatic fashion. He was a quiet man, with no discernible pastimes or interests outside of his family or his football club.

He loved both dearly and it's pleasing to know he had both on his mind in the hours before a sudden heart attack took him away from us.

His seat at the stadium remains inscribed with his name, and for playing his part in supporting this club for his entire life, and emboldening this community, his spirit lives on.

Some months after his passing, at an end-of-season celebration event, my brother had the opportunity to meet Akinfenwa. He explained my father's lifelong support of the club and how happy he was in his final moments thanks to the last-gasp goal Akinfenwa had scored. My brother thanked him for bringing our dad so much joy in his final few hours. The imposing 224-pound striker, nicknamed "The Beast," couldn't help but show his emotion as he listened intently to the story. "Stories like this are why I joined a family club like this," he said as he gave my brother a hug and wiped a tear from his eye.

The 1908 Olympic Marathon

SIR ARTHUR CONAN DOYLE

Editors' Note: Most know of British author Sir Arthur Conan Doyle as a master of mysteries, but the creator of Sherlock Holmes was also on hand to cover one of running history's biggest moments, Dorando Pietri's controversial finish at the marathon at the 1908 London Olympics. The modern Olympic Games were only twelve years old, but anticipation ran high around the race, which was then, and now, seen as a brutal test of endurance.

Pietri, running for Italy, did not lead during the first leg of the much-watched race, which began at Windsor Castle under the eyes of members of the British royal family and snaked through the streets of London. But in the second half, Pietri pushed to the front of the pack, only to hit the walls of dehydration and fatigue, villains known to countless runners through the ages. Whenever Pietri fell or lost his way on the course, at least once before a packed stadium of fans, umpires helped him back up and steered him back on track.

With assistance at least four different times, Pietri crossed the finish line first just ahead of American Johnny Hayes and basked in the win. Hayes later challenged Pietri's results, and the Italian was disqualified, thus making Hayes the somewhat anticlimactic gold medalist.

But now the great race is nearing us.

We are waiting, eighty thousand of us, for the man to appear, waiting anxiously, eagerly, with long turbulent swayings and headings which mark the impatience of the multitude. Through yonder doors he must come.

Every eye in the great curved bank of humanity is fixed upon the gap. What blazoning will show upon that dust-stained jersey—the red maple leaf, the blue and yellow, the Stars and Stripes, or the simple numbers of the Britons? Those figures on the board tell us nothing. It is the man who has a dash in him at the end who may head the field. He must be very near now, speeding down the street between the lines of shouting people. We can hear the growing murmur. Every eye is on the gap. And then at last he came.

But how different from the exultant victor whom we expected! Out of the dark archway there staggered a little man, with red running-drawers, a tiny boy-like creature. He reeled as he entered and faced the roar of the applause. Then he feebly turned to the left and wearily trotted round the track. Friends and encouragers were pressing round him.

Suddenly the whole group stopped. There were wild gesticulations. Men stooped and rose again. Good heavens, he has fainted: is it possible that even at this last moment the prize may slip through his fingers? Every eye slides round to that dark archway. No second man has yet appeared. Then a great sigh of relief goes up. I do not think that in all that great assembly any man would have wished victory to be torn at the last instant from this plucky little Italian. He has won it. He should have it.

Thank God, he is on his feet again—the little red legs going incoherently, but drumming hard, driven by a supreme will within. There is a groan as he falls once more, and a cheer as he staggers again to his feet. It is horrible, and yet fascinating, this struggle between a set purpose and an utterly exhausted frame. Again, for a hundred yards, he ran in the same furious and yet uncertain gait. Then again he collapsed, kind hands saving him from a heavy fall.

He was within a few yards of my seat. Amid stooping figures and groping hands I caught a glimpse of the haggard, yellow face, the glazed and expressionless eyes, the lank dark hair streaked across the brow. Surely he is done now. He cannot rise again.

From under the archway has darted the second runner, Hayes, Stars and Stripes on his breast, going gallantly well within his strength. There is only twenty yards to do if the Italian can do it. He staggered up, no trace of intelligence upon his set face, and again the red legs broke into their strange automatic amble.

Will he fall again? No, he sways, he balances, and then he is through the tape and into a score of friendly arms. He has gone to the extreme of human endurance. No Roman of the prime ever bore himself better than Dorando of the Olympics of 1908. The great breed is not yet extinct.

We owe a special thank-you to the Public Domain Review *(publicdomainreview.org) and the* Daily Mail *for bringing our attention to Doyle's track and field journalism dispatch.*

Requiem for the Ivory Coast: An Anatomy of Greece's Last-Minute Penalty

ROWAN RICARDO PHILLIPS

I, too, dislike it. . . .

Reading it, however, with a perfect contempt for it, one discovers in

it, after all, a place for the genuine.

—MARIANNE MOORE

Ivory Coast conceded a penalty to Greece in the final moments of a tied game that Greece needed to win to continue on in the 2014 World Cup and that the Ivory Coast only needed to keep as it was, level at a goal apiece, to make it out of Group C. This you know, and will remember. But if you happen to forget, the highlights will remind you: they'll show you the first-half goal the Ivory Coast served up on a platter for the Greeks—a mishit and rather foolish short back pass by Cheick Tioté deep in his own half—and that

Greece hit the woodwork three times; and then the dénouement came in the form of that penalty. Yet, what seems to have already faded from the telling story is that minute just prior to the penalty: the 90th minute. Aristotle, in his definition of tragedy, called this the *peripeteia*, reversal of fortune, the twist. Greece, in desperate need of a goal and appearing now to be short of ideas, lines up to take a free kick about 25 meters from the Ivorian goal. The kick is dreadful, hurtling directly into the wall of Ivorian players. The rebound falls to Solomon Kalou and, with space opening up ahead of him, he carries the ball forward into space and then, as that space quickly closes (a Greek specialty, an almost automated movement to defend even in moments when all seems lost), Kalou shows bravery and intelligence by releasing the ball wide to his teammate advancing toward the Greek goal. Greece had pressed the majority of their players forward for the failed free kick and, never speed merchants to begin with, couldn't get back and cover—suddenly Ivory Coast, now entering the final strokes of the game, enjoyed a rare two-on-two opportunity descending down on the Greek goal. The game at this point should have been liquidated: you score; or coax a foul out of one of the two exposed defenders; or you stretch the play out and keep the ball, forcing the Greeks to come back in numbers, and hence distance themselves from your goal, in an attempt to recuperate the ball as time mercilessly ticks away.

But what happened next was the disaster before the disaster for the Ivory Coast and the lifeline the Greeks so dearly needed. Zeus arranging pieces on the gameboard, Athena whispering something in someone's ear. The Ivorian player providing the supporting run off the ball, Yaya Touré, their star player, maintained a lane right down the center of the pitch as his teammate advanced on his left. It was a stubborn run by Touré. He was too close to his teammate. This meant that the second Greek defender was able to cover both Ivory Coast players at once, squaring up against one while shadowing the other. Touré wanted his goal: it would have been the moment of glory and relief; the game would have been salted away. But Touré—in search of a goal, wanting to be near the goal—made defending the play infinitely easier. As they say, it's a cruel game.

And then, suddenly, the great error: two more green jerseys joined in on the breakaway.

For a moment, I closed my eyes. What had started as a two-on-two had now become a four-on-two. Pointless running toward the wrong goal in search of a goal and a celebration. The play inevitably broke down. Touré, a player of great hierarchy, received a pass despite his bad positioning and after struggling to control the ball and make a little room for himself let go a feeble shot as he corkscrewed himself into the ground; the captain, exhausted and disappointed, stayed down; the other three Ivorians who had advanced now were out of position, stranded and unsure of what to do, where they should be. As the Greeks now had the ball and attempted to go forward with it the three Ivorian players who had advanced and were, unlike Yaya, still on their feet and likely sensing finally that they had strayed too far afield, now began to pressure the ball, hoping to rattle the Greeks into a loss of possession—which they didn't. The ball gets behind them. A Greek attacker receives a pass to the left of the Ivorian area.

At this point all is lost.

Ivory Coast is now short in numbers, stretched, and in being stretched unable to communicate effectively. Greeks flood the Ivory Coast goal, a few more look to support the left flank, a few more stop just short of the top edge of the area to provide passing angles for the player on the ball. The Ivorian defenders, who had never left their position, have it right: guard the men in the box. Three defenders mark three Greeks waiting in front of the goal for a chance. But now two more Greeks enter the area, streaking by Ivorian midfielders who were trotting back to stand in some seemingly semi-responsible defensive position . . . two don't even bother to do that. It's now some semblance of a four-on-four in the box. Yaya Touré's brother, Kolo, a natural defender, heads away a weak Greek pass lifted toward the Ivorian goal. The ball flies away from the Ivorian goal but finds another Greek player who waits and then passed the ball into inviting space on the left flank. Kolo's man takes the space, steadies himself under the ball. Kolo is forced to chase him. Now there are only two defenders in the box.

The pass is a rehearsed pass, the pass you make again and again from when you start playing when you're four or six and still make in practice when you run drills. In this situation it's the only pass that exists: diagonal, hard, and right to the penalty spot. The two Ivorian defenders have been pushed back toward their own goal, defending the most advanced Greek attackers. There should be at least six other Ivorians in the box. Six at the very least.

There are two.

Space should be the obsession now. They are in No Man's Land. The pass hums toward to the penalty spot as though it has a magnet in it and the white dot on the field is made of iron. It bullets past midfielder Serey Die, who rather seems strangely seems surprised by its presence. But the other Ivorian in No Man's Land, Giovanni Sio, who was loitering at the top of the box right next to where the once waiting now pouncing Greek player had been, luckless Giovanni Sio now gets it. He is a forward. He recognizes that pass. He's been on the receiving end of them. But now he's defending, misplaced and late in his recognition—he's out of time. He takes the step he should have taken six seconds ago.

It was a penalty. Full stop. Replay it. Question the decision. Rue the moment. Curse or praise the circumstance. Make your allusions to Greek gods and myths. Take this new crushing and definitive loss by an African team as a synecdoche of African football. Admit you were or are thinking about what an opportunity playing Costa Rica would have been or will be. Dread another ninety minutes of football as a war of attrition. Be happy that a team that is going to play from the first whistle to the final one, no matter what type of football they play. Think it a sad end for a golden generation. Think it a happy ending for a golden generation. Whatever you do, think about it. It's the why of what happened, but it won't make the highlights. You may not see it again. It's already gone.

This piece was originally published in the June 24, 2014, issue of The New Republic.

The "Dewey Defeats Truman" of Sports

JAMES ANDREW MILLER

Funny thing about failure. Once you've sampled it enough times, failure can become placating, perhaps soothing. It can even take on its own quality of prominence.

That's certainly the case when it comes to failure in sports. The longer a losing streak, the grander the grandeur, and the greater the greatness once the streak finally ends.

Assuming it ever does.

Philadelphia Phillies fans ruefully knew a lot about losing. They were unwitting, unwilling experts.

Imagine: From 1918 to 1948—three decades—the Phillies had only *one* winning season, finishing dead last in the National League in 1958, '59, '60, and '61—which they accomplished by pulling off a twenty-three-game losing streak, an all-time major-league record for losing. Somehow, the very next year, the Phillies won thirty-four more games and managed to finish with a winning season: going 81-80. 1963 saw continued improvement, with the Phils finishing 87-75 and coming in fourth.

Nevertheless, in advance of the 1964 season, when 232 Baseball Writers' Association of America members answered a query from *The Sporting News*, a scant ten picked Philadelphia to win the pennant. Phillies fans braced themselves for yet another season of dread and despair.

I remember those days with heartbreaking affection. My family lived in the Philadelphia suburbs, and I was just old enough to have fallen in love with baseball. We had come from New York; family and friends there seemed to be living on a different planet when it came to baseball. They started their seasons either euphoric about having won the previous World Series, or revengeful over the indignation of having somehow lost it. From 1947 to 1964, the Yankees missed the World Series only three times—1948, 1954, and 1959. Success was a starting point; championships never had to be only a dream. Phillies fans had no such legacy. The team was named in 1890, and there had been only *one* previous World Series appearance—a losing effort to the Boston Red Sox way back in 1915.

Picture what it was like for all of us on September 20, 1964, when our Phillies, our sad, luckless Phillies, found themselves with a mighty six-and-a-half-game lead over the St. Louis Cardinals with only twelve games to go. Simply put, it was a feeling Phillies fans had never experienced before. It was our city's everything. Everyone was talking about the team; wherever you went, they were the topic of conversation. The Phils were on top of the world, and so were we.

The Phillies had a different look and sound than in the previous, losing years. An eighteen-year-old and a thirty-six-year-old were on the roster. Key players' names seemed almost holy, even to nonbaseball fans living in and around Philadelphia: Richie Allen, Tony Gonzalez, Tony Taylor, Wes Covington, Clay Dalrymple, Cookie Rojas, and standout Johnny Callison, who was among the best hitters in the league, finishing the season with 31 home runs and 104 RBI, and coming in second in MVP voting. The pitching staff was led by Jim Bunning (who had already recorded the first regular-season perfect game since 1922), Chris Short, and Art Mahaffey. And the man who was engineering this surprise of a season, Phillies manager Gene Mauch, had become widely recognized as a legendary leader and strategist.

In an era when the National League winner automatically advanced to the World Series, the Phillies lead was so commanding that Major League Baseball gave the team permission to print World Series tickets before the regular season was over, only the third time in MLB history that this had been allowed. Within hours, 90,000 tickets had already been *sold* to the "Phillies 1964 World Series." According to *Sports Illustrated*, by 8:00 A.M. the following morning, the North Philadelphia Station, which handles the Phillies' mail, has logged 52,500 requests. The tickets were printed in eight colors—green, red, purple, brown, orange, blue, yellow, and gray—and each ticket bore a picture of the Philadelphia skyline. The Warwick Hotel was taking no more reservations for early October and expected to handle $50,000 worth of guests for the Series.

One of the worst teams in National League history was now a shoo-in to play in the World Series. The entire city was giddy with suspense in anticipation of that first series pitch.

Then it came—not the pitch but something else, something unexpected. It started the very day after tickets were printed, September 21, 1964, and it would turn out to be one of those big, fat, fateful turning points that can drive people, and cities, absolutely nuts.

Indeed, it's still talked about now and then, and those memories often well up to the point of causing goose bumps.

Connie Mack Stadium. Philadelphia. Start time: 8:10 P.M. Monday, a school night. Your narrator was too young to be up at such an hour, and besides, he had no reason to be concerned about this particular game. It was just another day closer to the awesome World Series itself.

The game is tied, with two strikes and two outs. The crowd is relatively calm. Future Hall of Famer Frank Robinson is up at bat and utility player Chico Ruiz is at third base, pacing. And then something truly bizarre happens. Something totally unexpected. Ruiz all of a sudden makes a sloppy attempt to steal home—shocking not only the Phillies, but the Reds as well. Oh, Chico! What the hell got into you?!

Instantly, commentators refer to it as a moronic move,

but to everyone's surprise, the pitch goes wild and Ruiz scores what turns out to be the game's only run. The Reds have just beaten the unsinkable first-place Phillies.

It was only one game, but in subsequent interviews, players would declare that Ruiz's strange decision to steal, and the weird twist of fate that he succeeded, created a whole Twilight Zone of an evening. It would wind up shaking the players and Phillies fans to their core, and made them wonder, well, made them wonder what baseball, perhaps even life, is all about.

The play gave birth to a legend: "The Curse of Chico Ruiz."

And from then on, the team was a parable of horribles. Every facet of the game of baseball that could go wrong for the Phillies, did.

The next game, the shaken Phillies were blown out 9–2 by the Reds, and in the game after that, Vada Pinson of the Reds hit a home run to ensure a 6–4 win over the Phils. The next day, there was a creepy stillness in the air, the kind that precedes full-blown bedlam. Let's face it, no one in the city had experience with being in first place at this time of the year. Nor could anyone dare think the team was now in *a slide for the ages*. At this point, all those lucky enough to get those World Series tickets were no doubt clutching them within inches of their lives. Surely, Our Phillies would get back to their winning ways.

It sure-as-shootin' felt that way two days later, when Richie Allen tied the game against the Milwaukee Braves by hitting an inside-the-park home run and thereby sending the game into extra innings. Ah, the magic was back. But then, dammit, a throwing error by Dalrymple in the top of the twelfth cost Philadelphia the game. Cue the mournful music. The magic was gone again.

Shockingly, the Phillies proceeded to lose the next ten consecutive games (yes, ten), each somehow more bizarre and baffling than the next, in one of the great meltdowns/chokes/falls-from-grace in MLB history. Vince Lombardi once said, "Winning is habit. Unfortunately, so is losing."

We're not talking about sudden-and-horrific loss here; we were now watching a sickening season that looked like it had been choreographed by Dante. No one on the field or in the city for that matter held their head high after these daily defeats, the slow twisting of the knife wreaking havoc on every vertebra in every back. Each day for those two weeks, smiles seemed smaller, elation less elated, and fear more feverish. If you were a kid and loved this game nearly as much as summer itself, the gods were certainly testing you. Some days you'd try not to look at the standings in the paper, but on September 28, those brave Phillies fans who did look saw the Reds had a one-game lead in the National League over the Cardinals and a one-and-a-half-game lead over the Phillies.

Phillies shortstop and first baseman Rubén Amaro, who had optimistically invited his family to the World Series, sent a wrenching letter home: "Dear Papa and Mama, Something is wrong with the team. We are all defeated before we start playing. Nothing is right, we just lose games. I have no words to tell you what is wrong. You know by the papers that we are a losing team, but we will keep on fighting to the end. . . .

Perhaps I planned too far ahead when I asked you to come to Philadelphia."

Tim McCarver of the St. Louis Cardinals reflected, "Ballplayers are animalistic when they can smell the blood, and on the contrary, when you're leaking blood, you understand that the prowl is underway. Those are the laws of nature, and those, really, are the laws of baseball. When you can smell the blood, you do things that you wouldn't ordinarily do. You're better than you think you are. And when you're losing like that, you're worse than you really are."

In a critical three-game series, the Cardinals swept the Phillies and took the lead of the division. Meanwhile, the Reds hit their own potholes during a poor series in Pittsburgh.

On the last day of the season, October 4, 1964, the Reds and Cardinals had identical records: 92-69. The Phillies were one game back at 91-70. In order to survive, the Phillies had to hope for the first three-way tie in the history of the game. To pull that off, the Phillies had to win their game against the Reds, and needed the Cardinals to lose to the Mets. Jim Bunning pitched a shutout, and the Phils roared to a 10-0 victory. But the Mets couldn't deliver for Philadelphia. The Cardinals beat them 11-5, finishing the season a game in front of the Phillies and the Reds, thus winning the pennant and moving on to, yes, the World Series.

Are the crying towels back from the laundry yet?

In 1964, the Phillies managed to do the impossible, not once but twice: they staged perhaps the greatest comeback season in their history, which few had seen coming, but then, ended the season with the ugliest defeats.

Many fans blamed Mauch, claiming he tired out the pitching staff and made poor decisions with his lineup. *Sports Illustrated* relayed a scene at the Chase Hotel, which occurred the night the Phillies were eliminated: Just before closing time, footsteps were heard in the long corridor that opens onto the bar. It was Mauch, his raincoat slung over his shoulder. The room fell silent as everyone looked at him. "Would you like a drink?" a friend asked. "I'd like a million," he said, and somehow managed to smile.

In the 1964 World Series, the Cardinals beat the Yankees in seven games.

As for the city of brotherly love, it hung in there, waiting for that vaunted World Series championship, and hung, and hung. It was well-hung. It would be another twelve years before mythic Rocky Balboa ran up those fabled art museum steps to the delight of the world, and sixteen more years until the Phillies won their first World Series in 1980. The city had found baseball Valhalla at last. Praise be.

The hubris inherent in the decision to print up World Series tickets before the season had ended was, of course, noteworthy and nutworthy, historic and hysterical. When years later, I saw one of those tickets for sale at a fund-raiser for cancer research, I couldn't resist outbidding the others. Framed, the ticket cautions me against overconfidence, a "Dewey Defeats Truman" of sports, a reminder never to brag that your ocean liner is "unsinkable," and a kind of *memento mori* for the ego: even when you've got a comfortable lead, even if you've got a comfortable seat, you *must* remember.

Remember the Alamo, remember the Edsel, remember *Ishtar*, and remember that surest of sure things, the '64 Phillies. And whatever you do, do not count those mother-clucking chickens before they hatch. You never know when some cynical twist of fate—possibly disguised as a stolen base—will send your entire season right down the tube.

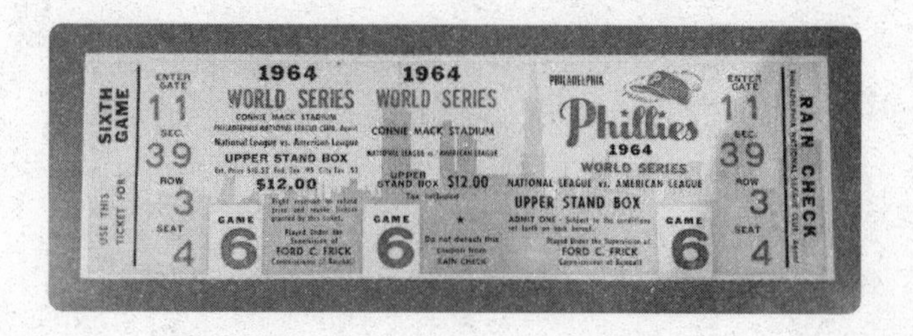

P.S. In 2007, the Mets broke the record for the biggest September collapse in Major League Baseball history when they blew a seven-game lead with seventeen games to play. The team that beat them? The Philadelphia Phillies.

Chasing Ashton Eaton: An Unintended Pursuit of the World's Greatest Athlete That No One Has Heard Of

JEREMY TAIWO, AS TOLD TO STEFANIE LOH

When I tell people I am an Olympic athlete, they sometimes imagine a life of wealth and fame. I will admit that I, too, thought Olympian status would confer some perks. But even after I returned from the 2016 Rio Olympics, I drove Uber and Lyft to make ends meet.

Looking back, I should have known what I was getting myself into. I'm the son of a two-time Olympian, and you've probably never heard of my father, either.

When I tell people that I'm an Olympic *decathlete*, I can see people recalibrate their reactions. I often get blank stares. A lot of people don't know what the decathlon is. I try to explain that the decathlon traditionally crowns the world's best all-around athlete, through a series of ten events: the 100-meter dash, the long jump, the shot put, the high jump, the 400-meter dash, the 110-meter hurdles, the discus, the pole vault, the javelin, and the 1,500-meter run. These days, though, the phrase "best athlete" is reserved for mainstream sports stars like LeBron James.

Making it to one Olympic Games does give you enough street cred to do some motivational speaking on the side. I sometimes do a little test and ask the audience how many people have heard of Ashton Eaton. These days, I'm pleasantly surprised if even half a dozen hands go up. I've grown accustomed to the silence now, but it used to come as a shock.

Eaton retired in 2017 as the greatest decathlete the world has ever seen, the most dominant of all time. He walked away from the sport with two Olympic gold medals and what was at the time the decathlon world record of 9,045 points. He also has two of the top three scores in decathlon history, the top four scores in heptathlon history, two world titles, and three world indoor titles to his name. I've spent my entire athletic career chasing him.

It's humbling to realize that no one has ever heard of the man whose records I can only dream of.

He is a friend, of sorts. We are competitors, but I identify with him. We're both fighting to distinguish ourselves in a sport that's not exactly high-profile. Plus, we come from similar backgrounds. We are both mixed-race natives of the Pacific Northwest—a region of the country acknowledged more for rain and salmon than as a hotbed of athleticism—and track stars who stuck close to home for college. He grew up in Bend, Oregon, and went to the University of Oregon, while I grew up just outside of Seattle and attended the University of Washington on an athletic scholarship. He's two years older than I, so our college careers overlapped in my first couple of seasons. In the Pac-10 (now the Pac-12), we raced each other on tracks all over the West Coast.

There is no question that chasing after him made me better in college. He showed me the standard to beat and pushed me to work harder every day. Still, I just didn't know at the time that I'd be competing against the best athlete the sport had ever seen. I sometimes wonder how much more hardware I might have bagged if I hadn't come into the sport two years after a once-in-a-generation decathlete rose to prominence. From the first meet we competed in together—the 2009 NCAA indoor nationals at the end of my freshman year at UW, Ashton's junior year at the Oregon—to the day he retired, I never once beat him in a full decathlon.

I've finished ahead of him in some events: usually the 1,500 meters, the shot put, and the high jump. But even on my best day, at the 2016 US Olympic Trials, I came in behind him.

It was maddening to finish so close to the top—again and again. I finished third at the 2009 Pac-10 championships, second in the 2010 Pac-10 championships, third at the 2013 USA outdoor nationals, second at the 2016 Olympic Trials, and eleventh at the 2016 Rio Olympics. Ashton stood atop the medal platform on every one of those occasions, wearing the gold medal that I so coveted.

For perspective, my 7,521 points at the 2010 Pac-10

championships would have won me a Big Ten title that year. My 8,425 points at the 2016 Olympic Trials would have been good enough for a bronze medal at the 2012 London Olympics.

But such is the plight of every decathlete who's ever shared a track with Ashton Eaton: he's *always* raised the bar—often to ethereal heights us mere mortals couldn't dream of touching.

What makes it even worse is that he's so darn *nice* about it. He's such a kind, genuine person that it's impossible to hate him. When I came in second at the Olympic Trials to qualify for a spot on my first-ever Olympic team in 2016—top three finishers make the squad—he gave me a big hug and said, "Hey, you're an Olympian, man." He seemed genuinely happy that for the first time ever, I would be competing right beside him at the Olympics. He's never territorial on the track, always quick to offer tape, snacks, or help to his fellow competitors. He's the kind of guy who goes on goodwill trips to Africa to help promote education and sponsor underprivileged children. He's just a good dude through and through.

On the track, being in the presence of greatness can either deflate you or motivate you. I chose to make it the latter, but I wasn't impervious to the former.

This sport is hard. It's borderline masochistic. It requires a perfectionist mind-set and involves hours upon hours of solitary training as you obsess over the three hundred thousand different ways you need to work to improve your results in so many different disciplines. So inevitably, there were days when I sat there and asked myself: *How crazy is it that someone with my same background is accomplishing the exact same things I want to accomplish?*

Often, it seemed as if life were mocking me, saying: *Here's everything you've ever wanted, Jeremy. We're going to put it in front of you and make it look equal parts attainable and impossible by giving it to the guy who came into it just ahead you. We've decided to empower him to accomplish all the things you want to do, and make it look effortless while he's doing it.*

On some metaphysical level, I wondered in my more insecure moments, was *my* desire somehow feeding *Ashton*? Was the hunger, will, and all the drive that I was channeling into the universe being shot out of the wrong torpedo tube?

Yet, therein lies the beauty of sports in its purest sense. Despite what the oddsmakers say, or what your competitors' résumés and career trajectories indicate, on any given day, you never know what will happen when you step up to that start line and dig in. That's what has kept me going over the last ten years. That's why, through seven major injuries, five surgeries, financial despair, and multiple maddening finishes behind Ashton, I've stuck with this sport and all the heartbreak that comes with it.

Through it all, I kept myself grounded with the knowledge that I could only be as good as I wanted to be. My input directly correlated to my output. I didn't have the mental or emotional energy to pay much attention to my competitors. I didn't follow other scores and never watched a second of the 2012 Olympics because I wasn't there. I dedicated every ounce of myself to my preparation because that's all I could control.

And while it might be hard for you to believe this, even though my track teammates and numerous coaches over the years continually tried to get me to consciously chase Ashton—his times, his records, his medals—I knew, deep inside, that I never wanted to be seen as the next Ashton Eaton. I always wanted to be seen only as Jeremy Taiwo.

Because my pursuit of Olympic glory has never been about chasing Ashton Eaton. It was a lifelong personal quest to chase my father, two-time Nigerian Olympian Joseph Taiwo.

I GREW UP IN the shadow of my Olympian father's greatness.

Years later, I would come to realize that any pressure I'd felt to live up to him had really been self-imposed. But throughout my childhood, Dad and his athletic legacy loomed large. To me, he was a giant among men.

Dad wasn't one to regale us with tales of his athletic accomplishments, and I don't think I ever saw a video of him triple-jumping in the Olympics until my college track coach showed me an old clip one day at UW. But I'd always held my father in the highest regard.

He was a stern authority figure and a man of few words—the kind of guy who could drive forty-five minutes with no sound but smooth jazz playing in the background and would make no attempt at conversation with the eager-to-please teenage boy riding shotgun next to him. Dad seldom offered words of praise or affirmation, which, in hindsight, probably contributed to the development of my perfectionist nature and my fervent desire to earn his respect. But he showed his affection for his kids in other ways. When I was growing up, he worked a 6:00 A.M. to 2:00 P.M. shift as an IT help desk analyst at Nordstrom so that he could pick up my brother and me after school and chauffeur us to our various extracurricular activities. He coached me in track and field at my high school, and he and my mother raised us in line with the culture of his strict Nigerian upbringing.

My father was born in Ibadan, Nigeria, in 1959, and he displayed his athletic prowess early on. He was the fastest kid in the neighborhood, and by elementary school, he had established such a formidable reputation that the only kid willing to challenge him to a footrace was his twin sister, Ololade. When he wasn't outrunning the competition, Dad spent his afternoons after school high-jumping buck naked against the neighborhood kids. In the pre–Under Armour era, it was apparently easier to clear great heights when you didn't have any clothes getting in your way.

These naked high-jumping escapades led to Dad trying the long jump.

When he discovered the triple jump in high school, he realized that jumping, not running, would be his meal ticket out of Nigeria. He knew he'd have to leave Nigeria to get the proper training to hone his talents, and so he set his sights on moving to the United States. Dad's wish came true in 1981 when he received an athletic scholarship to compete at Washington State University. There, he met my part-Colombian mother, Irene Botero, and he developed the triple-jumping skills that would ultimately take him to the 1984 and 1988 Olympic Games. My parents were married in the fall of 1988, and soon after, my dad got his green card and became a US citizen. I was born in 1990 and grew up in Seattle. But we lived in Denver for a few years when I was a boy, and while there, I watched my dad train for one final Olympic Games, this time as a member of the US track team. In doing so, he unknowingly planted the seeds of my Olympic dream.

Unfortunately, due to injury, he did not make the US team. But watching my father come up short on that final attempt to represent his chosen homeland at the Olympics only contributed to the formulation of my lifelong ambition.

We moved back to Seattle in 1996, and I recall sitting in my grandparents' living room that summer watching the opening ceremonies for the 1996 Olympics on TV, completely spellbound. Right then, I decided that for me to ever be worthy of his respect, I, too, would have to someday compete in the Olympic Games.

WE WERE WAITING IN the holding area to walk into Maracanã Stadium in Rio in on August 5, 2016, when it started to dawn on me that I was finally about to experience the event I'd watched reverently on television every four years throughout my childhood.

As the American athletes assembled for the Opening Ceremony, I had strategically situated myself toward the front of our delegation, less than ten feet behind flag bearer Michael Phelps. I felt like a kid at the zoo gawking at a collection of beautiful, exotic animals as I stared appreciatively at the diverse array of country-themed outfits worn by the athletes from different countries. As the lines of colorfully dressed athletes streamed into the stadium, I wondered how Team USA would be received.

This was the summer of 2016. At home, the Republican nominee for president, Donald Trump, was stirring up heated anti-immigrant sentiment. A Black Lives Matter movement was gaining traction. There seemed to be a debate as to who could call themselves "real" US citizens. At least that's how it felt to me, the mixed-race son of a Nigerian father and a part-Colombian mother, and a first-generation American. I wasn't quite sure how the rest of the world would greet us.

Any fears about a potentially hostile reception from the Brazilian crowd melted away as I jogged into the stadium and my ears were accosted by the rumbling roar of seventy-eight thousand people chanting, "U-S-A. U-S-A." Whatever qualms I had myself about representing a nation that wasn't quite sure whether to accept me disappeared, at least for that moment. As I absorbed the rabid energy of the crowd cheering around me, I felt like an ancient gladiator getting psyched to fight.

That's when it finally sunk in: They were cheering for *me*! I'd done it. I was an athlete at the Olympic Games. I was walking in the very ceremony I'd watched so often as a child while thinking, *I could do that, I could get there.*

It was both absurdly surreal and thoroughly satisfying to live out my dreams in real time. With every step I took as I strode proudly through that stadium, I felt the centuries of tradition underfoot and allowed myself to luxuriate in the knowledge that I'd finally joined this elite club of supremely athletic humans. It made everything I'd had to endure to get here completely worth it.

I don't know where Ashton was at that moment, and I didn't care. This wasn't about him. All I cared about was being present in the moment of my dreams, taking it all in with wide eyes, an open heart, and a smile on my face. This was truly the one moment in my life where I had no intentions beyond just existing and being grateful to be there.

As has so often been the case before big moments throughout my athletic career, I was injured going into the Olympics. I'd pulled a muscle in my groin after the Olympic Trials, and that severely impacted my ability to train for the Olympic Games. Heading into Rio, I wasn't able to practice discus or javelin, I was limited in the hurdles, and I'd had one high-jump practice, one pole vault practice and a shot put practice.

The Games came at a particularly trying time in my life. My girlfriend and I weren't doing well, and I was in a messy, drawn-out dispute with my sponsor. I'd been stressed out all year with trying to raise enough money to, first, go to Olympic Trials, and then to get to the Games. Then, after finally making the US team, I felt so much pressure to live up to this golden chance that I'd painstakingly earned.

I'd finished Olympic Trials second behind Ashton in Eugene, Oregon, tallying a career-high 8,425 points. For two spectacular days at Hayward Field, the heavens aligned and I put away all concerns about injury, legacy, money, and expectations to turn in the best performance of my entire career.

Through the first four events at Trials, I actually led the field, ahead even of the world record holder, Ashton. At the end, after running the race of my life in the penultimate event: the 1,500 meters, I stood on the podium, next to Ashton, heart swelling as the silver medal was placed around my neck.

I looked out into the stands and saw my parents waving excitedly. My father was smiling. He knew, and I knew, that I'd finally done what he never managed to do: make the US Olympic track team—often considered the most difficult team in the world to make due to the sheer depth of talent in this country.

In that moment, I was so immensely proud of what I'd accomplished, and if I'd been able to train the way I wanted leading up to the Olympics, I truly believe I might have had a shot at the bronze medal.

But getting injured before the biggest meet of my life forced me to slow down, accept my fate, and resolve to live in the moment. It helped me let go of some of the pressure I'd exerted on myself and just compete. I knew I wasn't going to be at my best in Rio, but I was determined to honor the journey by at least finishing. That mental change in directive was freeing. From that point on, when I walked out onto the track before every event, I was infused with an otherworldly sense of calm. *This is the Olympics,* I'd think. *It doesn't get any better than this.*

The high jump has always been my best event in the decathlon, and it's usually when I'm at my most relaxed and completely in my element.

While getting ready to clear a bar in the high jump, I waved my arms around to get the crowd going, and that's when I looked up into the stands and found my parents. They were standing next to each other looking happy and proud and content. Together, they gave me a thumbs-up.

That might have been one of the best moments of my life: my father, sitting at the Olympic Games, watching his son in a Team USA jersey competing in the decathlon, and flashing me a thumbs-up. It was one of the few times in my life that he's truly acknowledged my accomplishments for what they are instead of simply urging me on to greater heights. In that moment, I didn't care where I finished or who I finished behind.

Ashton won the decathlon the next day. I finished eleventh in a field of twenty-five and might have been disappointed if I hadn't already realigned my expectations with reality.

Six months later, Ashton retired. When I heard the news, I thought about how, for the first time in my career, the world's greatest decathlete was no longer one of my direct competitors.

But it was difficult to get excited about that when my own future in the sport was also in doubt.

Right after the Olympics, I found myself drifting, uncertain about whether I wanted to train for another quad to qualify for Tokyo 2020. The constant slew of injuries I'd dealt with since college had worn me down. Over six years since my junior season at UW, I'd endured and overcome one physical ailment after another: Tommy John surgery on my elbow, a sports hernia, and nagging, long-suffering issues with my knee, my hamstring, and my groin. To compound matters, after the Olympics, I was injured yet again. This time, an adductor issue kept me from training through most of 2017.

I was sick of the constant grind of recuperation and rehabilitation, punctuated by intense training, and the constant worry about how I was going to pay for my competitions and daily living expenses. My Olympic experience had not yielded any sort of financial windfall. I was still working at a cryotherapy place and driving rideshare cars. Did I really want to keep this up for one more shot at an Olympic medal in four years?

Then, in March 2018, I surprised myself by winning the U.S. indoor heptathlon title. Briefly, I let myself think that 2020 might be my chance, with Ashton out of the picture.

But the Italian Decathlon a month later brought clarity in the form of yet another injury. My Achilles tendon started throbbing ominously after I ran the 100 meters and the first thought that entered my head was, "Jeremy, you're not in a position to pay for an expensive Achilles surgery."

I thought I was done. My heart wasn't quite in it anymore.

The idea of enduring yet another round of rehab, then starting over, getting back into shape, and putting everything else in my life on hold to chase the Olympics again suddenly seemed more exhausting than it was worth. I didn't have anything left to prove to anyone.

My desire to push was gone.

Ashton was gone. Off to live out the rest of his life with his legacy already made. He wasn't there to chase any more. In his absence, I've realized it was never about him anyway.

The pressure I've put on myself all these years to live up to my father's legacy is gone.

I was done—or so I thought.

I took the next year off. Played some Aussie-rules football, competed on American Ninja Warrior, explored my options, and took it easy. But by spring 2019, I realized I was getting depressed because I wasn't working out. I missed having something big to work toward.

Then I ran into the new UW multis coach, Toby Stevenson, and he gushed about his talented young decathlete, Tim Duckworth, who was hoping to make Great Britain's team at the 2020 Olympics.

"I was thinking about reaching out to you to get someone for Tim to work out with," Toby said. "You're from UW, you're an Olympian; I'll write a program for you. Let's do this."

I mulled the proposition, then went back to Toby and told him I was in.

As an athlete, you have only so many viable years to compete. With an experienced, supportive multis coach in my backyard, and an eager young star to pit myself against in training every day, it seemed like no-brainer.

Let's do this. Let's go all out. One last go-around. A final hurrah.

Galiyeva-ed

CARLA CORREA

Roza Galiyeva was chosen to lose. Of course, you hear that gymnasts are "robbed" all the time—robbed of a medal, or robbed of their chance to compete, or even robbed of their childhoods. But Galiyeva? She really *was* robbed.

At the 1992 Olympic Games in Barcelona, few outside of the tight-knit world of gymnastics had heard of Galiyeva, a fifteen-year-old Uzbek, until her scores in a preliminary competition earned her a coveted spot in the women's all-around competition. Her joy was short-lived. The coaches for the Unified Team—most of the nations of the former Soviet Union were competing together one final time—falsely claimed that she was injured, so that her place could be handed to a teammate who did not qualify. That teammate, Tatiana Gutsu, ended up winning the gold medal by a mere .012 points over the American Shannon Miller. It was the tightest margin of victory ever in an Olympic all-around.

In Barcelona, Rozaliya Ilfovna Galiyeva was the youngest

and least experienced member of the Unified Team. These Olympics were the last in which these gymnasts would, as a unit, flaunt their dismantled superpower's athletic prowess. Since 1952 the Soviets had won the team title at every Games except the one they boycotted in 1984. They had also won the lion's share of the individual gymnastics medals. The dissolution of the USSR didn't change the lofty expectations. At Barcelona's Palau Sant Jordi Stadium the scoreboard displayed EUN (for Équipe Unifiée, Unified Team in French) instead of the International Olympic Country code of URS, and the Olympic banner and its colorful rings flew in place of the red Soviet flag, but Moscow still expected multiple medals, preferably gold, from its gymnasts.

Gutsu was a prematch favorite. But she had stepped off the balance beam during the preliminary competition, and Galiyeva had finished ahead of her in the standings, meaning that Galiyeva, not Gutsu, would vie for an all-around medal. At the end of the qualifications, Galiyeva can be seen on NBC footage briefly consoling a crying Gutsu.

Not so fast. A plan was swiftly put into motion: Galiyeva, who placed eighth among every gymnast that day, would not participate in further events. Her coaches said she had a knee injury. Fans were skeptical. Gutsu had finished ninth, but both women could not compete because of what is known as the "per country" rule, which handicaps the field in the interest of diversity. In 1992, only three women per nation could advance; by 2004, only two women could advance.

As was expected by the state, Galiyeva initially said

nothing publicly about the substitution. When Gutsu won the gold medal and the fame that came with it, Galiyeva still did not speak out. It was years before she confirmed that she had not been hurt. "Of course, I was very upset that Gutsu got to perform," she told NBC in 1996, just before she finally competed in an Olympic all-around, at the Atlanta Games. "But what could I do? And it wasn't my decision. It was the decision of [the] head coach. I couldn't do anything about it."

To be clear, no one in Barcelona actually thought Galiyeva could beat the top Romanians and Americans in the high-pressure all-around. She was largely untested in international competition, and her gymnastics was not as difficult as Gutsu's. As for the Unified Team, Galiyeva's hurt feelings were the least of its concerns. They were there to win.

Still, Galiyeva's sidelining made an impact—especially after NBC ran a segment during the 1996 Olympics, playing up the injustice for sympathetic American viewers. Among the sport's fans, Galiyeva's name became a verb: Galiyeva had been "Galiyeva-ed." After that, it seemed that whenever a gymnast had qualified for a prestigious competition, only to have the spot ripped away by adults or bureaucrats who thought that another gymnast, who did not perform as well, deserved it more, the gymnast was said to be "Galiyeva-ed."

Galiyeva, of course, was not the first gymnast to be "Galiyeva-ed," nor would she be the last.

Head coaches can still cheat the "per-country rule" by faking an athlete's injury or otherwise blacklisting a qualified gymnast. In fact, in 1996, the very year that NBC aired the story of Galiyeva's tribulations, the Romanian gymnast Alexandra Marinescu qualified to the Olympic all-around, only to be replaced by her teammate Simona Amânar. Her coach's reason, as reported in the media, was that Marinescu did not "work hard enough."

NBC may have liked to suggest that Galiyeva was a "sacrificial lamb," as John Tesh put it in the 1996 segment. "Medals meant honor," Tesh said. "What was fair was not even discussed." What he did not mention at the time was that the gymnast Kim Kelly was left off Bela Karolyi's American squad in 1992, despite placing sixth at the Olympic Trials and initially being named to the team. "I trained my whole life to have people just ruin everything," Kim later told the *New York Times*.

At the 1996 Olympics, Galiyeva competed for Russia. This time, she again qualified in eighth place—and got to compete in the all-around. She finished a disappointing seventh.

The Kyrgios Enigma

LOUISA THOMAS

Nick Kyrgios, the twentieth-ranked tennis player in the world, stepped to the baseline. He briskly bounced the ball and rocked forward to begin his serve, his arms swinging. He has a narrow waist and strong shoulders, a greyhound's look, and a greyhound's air of languid indifference. Kyrgios, a twenty-two-year-old Australian, is the only active player ever to defeat Roger Federer, Rafael Nadal, and Novak Djokovic in their first meetings; he has beaten Nadal and Djokovic twice, in fact, and came within a few points of a second victory over Federer earlier this year. "I think Nick is the most talented player since Roger jumped on the scene," Paul Annacone, a former coach of Federer and Pete Sampras, has said. Kyrgios is also the most mercurial. Jon Wertheim, the executive editor of *Sports Illustrated*, once called him "tennis' id."

It was the second round of the Open Parc Auvergne-Rhône-Alpes Lyon, a small tournament in the run-up to the

French Open. There was a charge in the air, as there always is when Kyrgios plays. He is known for his spectacular shots: he has the skill and the imagination of Federer or John McEnroe. His matches have also featured epic displays of ranting, racquet-wrecking, and trash-talking. Kyrgios once flagrantly tried to lose a match, bopping in a serve like a beginner, and starting to walk off the court before it bounced. At some point in almost every match, he tends to do something brilliant—or he snaps.

Twisting, eyes wide, he opened his shoulders and tossed the ball. Then he reared up and whipped his racquet toward the toss. It is an efficient, brutally effective motion. In a match in March, Kyrgios aced Djokovic, the greatest returner in the history of the game, twenty-five times in two sets. He hits flat serves more than a hundred and forty miles per hour. He slices the ball so that it skids the line. He can put on so much spin that the ball arcs in at eighty-four miles per hour and then leaps up above the returner's head, as if the ground were a trampoline.

Across the net from Kyrgios was Nicolas Kicker, a twenty-four-year-old Argentine who is ranked ninety-fourth in the world. Serving at 5–2, 40–15, Kyrgios already had five aces. This serve, down the T, made it six. His forward momentum carried him toward his chair, as if that were his destination all along.

It was a lovely afternoon—mid-May, the golden hour—but something seemed wrong. Kyrgios winced and grabbed his hip. An old injury had flared up in Madrid two weeks earlier; he'd been forced to withdraw from a tournament in Rome. He started to shorten points, to limit the strain on his hip. He hit drop shots from well behind the baseline which died on the net. He went for aces, on both first and second serves. Kyrgios, who has an unusually aggressive game, often uses such tactics to great effect. But as the match wore on he appeared to be exhibiting not strategy but impatience. After one error, he bounced his racquet in disgust and caught it on the handle. The crowd murmured expectantly. They were ready for a meltdown. Instead, he bounced the racquet and caught it again, and again, as if to distract himself.

Kicker, serving for the set, hit a drop shot that hung in the air on the bounce. Kyrgios has tremendous speed; ordinarily, he could have covered the ground. Instead, he took only one step into the court, ceding the point. A few minutes later, he served and rushed the net, letting Kicker's return fly by him; the ball landed well inside the lines. Point, Kicker. Down set point, with a second serve, Kyrgios went for the ace. It clipped the top of the net. Double fault. Kyrgios spent the changeover flipping a little Evian water bottle.

Kicker started swinging more freely. His serve got more pop. He hit several successful drop shots, testing Kyrgios's sore hip. It started to look like the final at Roland Garros on Kicker's side of the net, and an exhibition match on Kyrgios's. Kyrgios ran around his forehand to hit a tweener—a between-the-legs shot—from the doubles alley, which Kicker easily blocked back into the open court. When Kicker broke his serve and took command of the set, Kyrgios slammed his racquet into the dirt. His hip seemed increasingly to bother him. So, perhaps, did his spirit; his grandfather, who helped rear him, had died a few weeks before. In the end, Kicker easily took the second and third sets, beating a top-fifty player for the first time. Kyrgios trudged to the net to shake his hand.

Half an hour after the match, I was waiting for the elevator in the lobby of my hotel, when I heard Kyrgios request a new room key. He was still in his kit: black shorts, a magenta Nike top, shoes smeared with ochre clay. His beard was trimmed tight along his jawline, his dark hair shaved on the sides of his head and sculpted on top like a flame.

He stared at his phone as he shuffled to the elevator. As he stepped inside, he looked up. We had met the previous day, and he sounded surprisingly cheerful as he greeted me.

"Sorry about the match," I said.

He gave a quick, harsh laugh, and then his voice lightened. "It's all right. It's not a big deal," he said.

He stepped out of the elevator, and I watched the doors close behind his slumped shoulders. There are message-board threads dedicated to Kyrgios's posture, with dozens of comments debating whether the curvature of his upper back requires surgery, interferes with his hormone circulation, or is a faker's lazy pose.

Kyrgios says that he doesn't want to be Federer. So what does he want? When you're a tennis player who claims not to like playing tennis, when half the world (including most of Australia) seems to have an opinion of your character, and when you're twenty-two years old, the answer can be complicated.

People tend to tell one of two stories about Kyrgios. Either he is a talented kid who is wasting his gift with a bad attitude and a terrible work ethic, or he is a talented kid who has struggled, sometimes severely, with his motivation, but who is maturing. A column in the Sydney *Morning Herald* was headlined "Nick Kyrgios Is a National Embarrassment." Other people believe that he could be the future of men's tennis.

"I think he has the most talent of anyone twenty-five and under," Brad Gilbert, an ESPN commentator and Andre Agassi's former coach, told me. "If you put the total package around him"—coaches, trainers, focused practice sessions, strenuous training blocks—"and he embraced that, I would be shocked if he didn't win multiple slams and become top two in the world."

"People tell me I need to change, but it has to come from me," Kyrgios told me before playing Kicker in Lyon. We were sitting in the hotel restaurant, with his agent, John Morris, in the lull between breakfast and lunch. Kyrgios wore long blue shorts and a Vince Carter jersey with a chain tucked into the neck. He drank a tiny glass of orange juice.

"I don't think I want it enough," Kyrgios said. He shook his head and said it again. Perhaps he was tired. His beloved Celtics had had a playoff game against Cleveland the night before, and he had been up at 3:00 A.M. to watch. "The thing about tennis life is that it's the same thing every day," Kyrgios said. "You train. You come back to the hotel. You get treatment. You eat. You sleep. You get up." It is unglamorous and exhausting, a life spent half in airports and hotels, thousands of miles from home. Almost every trip is punctuated, often early, with a loss. Some players orient themselves by the familiarity of their routines. Not Kyrgios: he gets homesick, injured, and bored. He wants to be playing basketball; he'd rather be fishing; he misses his dogs, his girlfriend, his family, his friends.

Other young players, such as Dominic Thiem and Alexander Zverev, may be safer bets to win a slam soon. Zverev, a twenty-year-old German, recently beat Djokovic in Rome, becoming the youngest player to win a Masters title since Djokovic himself, in 2007. I asked Kyrgios whether Zverev's win motivated him. "I'm incredibly happy for him," he said, and it was obvious that he meant it. "But I don't know if it motivates me. I didn't feel, as soon as he won, Man, I'm going to go train, or anything. He won a tournament. It's good, but it's more weeks on the road where we're going to play tennis matches, and that's it."

Many people assume that Kyrgios is in denial about his ambition. "I think deep down, in his own way, he's becoming more professional," Paul McNamee, a retired Australian player and a former C.E.O. of the Australian Open, told me. "But to admit that and to fail—he would not cope with that, maybe." Kyrgios resists that analysis. "Some days, I'm really good," he said. "I like going out on the practice court and training with my mates. But I don't know about fully engaging and giving everything to it. It's just a game. It's just a sport. It's such a small part of my life."

I asked Kyrgios why he doesn't quit. "I'd rather be doing that than working at Chipotle or something," he said. "For me, it's an easy way to make money. I'm just hitting a ball over a net." He added, "Of course, I've grown up with it. It's a part of me. It's all I really know how to do."

Kyrgios got up from his chair; he had a doubles match in a few hours. I was left with Morris, a compact Englishman with a thoughtful look. "He doesn't do it for the money," Morris said. "He doesn't know what he has in the bank. He's a competitor. He's always competing."

"So why does he sometimes stop trying to win?" I asked.

"I don't know. He's a bit of an enigma. I wish I knew. I think Nick probably wishes he knew more about it, too."

KYRGIOS'S FIRST LOVE WAS basketball. He spent countless hours watching *Space Jam* and playing the video game *NBA Live*. Eventually, he persuaded his parents to get a cable-TV package that included NBA games. He'd wake up early to watch the Celtics and then go outside to shoot baskets, pretending that he was Paul Pierce. When he was fourteen, he was selected for a regional team. "I love the game. I love the sound of the basketball court," he told me. "I love the team environment."

He also played tennis, beginning group lessons when he was seven. "My mum wanted us to participate," his sister,

Halimah, explained. Nick's father, George, a housepainter, came from Greece as a child; his mother, Nill, a computer engineer, was born in Malaysia. They reared three children, Christos, Halimah, and Nicholas, in a split-level house in a suburb of Canberra. George's parents and Nill's mother lived nearby and looked after the kids during the day. Halimah recalled that Nick, the youngest, "was just a cute little thing—very competitive, but I think that comes from Christos. When you're the youngest, you're always fighting to be better than the rest."

He was best at tennis. A local coach, Andrew Bulley, recognized Kyrgios's talent and started giving him private lessons. He hated to practice. "As soon as it became boring, he'd lose interest," Bulley recalled. "He wanted scoring." Kyrgios, who was overweight and asthmatic, couldn't run well, which meant that he had to develop an original game. When he was out of position, he learned to hit winners off his heels or the back foot, using his loose arm to generate speed. He scraped deep shots off the bounce or delicately half-volleyed them instead of moving his feet. He did everything he could to play a point on his terms. "I had to work out way more to be more aggressive than the average player," Kyrgios said.

By the time Kyrgios was ten, he was playing in Australia's twelve-and-under national championships. By his early teens, he was travelling to Europe and Asia to play tournaments. Tennis is one of the most expensive sports to play at an elite level—travel and coaching can easily cost tens of thousands of dollars per year—and Kyrgios's talent strained the family's finances. Halimah recalled, "My parents had to decide, 'Do we put in the money, all the money we have, to trust that it's going to get somewhere?'" When Kyrgios was fifteen, Tennis Australia, the country's governing body for the sport, and the Australian Institute of Sport, a national training center, offered him help in funding his career and a spot at the A.I.S. "My dad kind of just came out and said, 'What's easier to make it in, in Australia, playing basketball or tennis?' Obviously, I knew the answer was tennis," Kyrgios said.

At the A.I.S., he was miserable at first. He liked the camaraderie of the training center, but he missed basketball, and he hated the repetition required on the court. Still, his game got better, his diet improved, and, when he was fifteen, he had a growth spurt that left him lean, even skinny. At seventeen, in 2013, Kyrgios won the junior title at the Australian Open. The following year, he faced Rafael Nadal, the No. 1 player in the world, at Wimbledon. On the first point of the match, Kyrgios hit an ace down the T; Nadal barely had time to flinch. Kyrgios aced him thirty-seven times, hitting seventy winners in all. At 3–3 in the second set, he flicked his racquet behind his back and through his legs. The ball barely cleared the net, landing just inside the line. The tweener became his signature shot. Kyrgios won the match in four sets. He dropped his racquet and held his head in his hand. Morris told me, "You don't see that same joy, sheer joy, anymore."

Kyrgios won ten matches in slams before he won two in regular events. Off the main stage, he began to struggle with the demands of the tour. At the moment when most top players build up an entourage of coaches, physiotherapists, and trainers, Kyrgios split with one coach and then another, and struck out on his own. "Every coach I had tried to tame me, tried to make me play more disciplined, tried to make me do drills," he told me. "All through my career, there were people trying to tell me to play a more normal style of tennis." But, he went on, "I've just been kind of playing on instinct. I feel like it's been successful, so I don't know why there's a good reason to stop that."

Not having a coach meant that there was less accountability in practice. In Lyon, I watched him hit with another Aussie, Matt Reid, two days before the match against Kicker. Kyrgios did it his way. Warming up, he entertained the little crowd of kids gathered at the chain-link fence by punctuating his grunts with the names of other players ("Dominic UH Dominic UH Thiem EH-UH Jo-Willy UH Jo-Wilfried UH"). He started hitting one-handed topspin backhands, a shot I'd never seen him hit in a match. He and Reid began to play out the points. "Fucking move your legs, you shit!" Kyrgios yelled at himself. Another backhand miss: "Make it!" A few shots later, he was smiling.

Those who know Kyrgios talk about his easy nature and his sense of humor. Yet he became prone to smashing racquets, arguing with umpires, and berating ball kids. He once prolonged a changeover at Wimbledon by theatrically changing his socks. At many tournaments, he racked up thousands of dollars in fines for unsportsmanlike conduct. Most appalling, he told Stan Wawrinka during a match that a friend had "banged" his girlfriend.

Last fall, in Shanghai, Kyrgios had his episode of openly trying to lose a match. "I was just done," he told me. "I was, like, 'Next week, I get to go home, and the only thing that's holding me back is this match.'" He was fined twenty-five thousand dollars and suspended for three months, a penalty that was reduced to eight weeks after he agreed to see a psychologist. "Tennis, for me—it's a completely different me," he said. "The person I am on the court is not who I am off the court."

KYRGIOS IS HARDLY THE first to struggle with the warping pressure of being on tour and alone on the court. Suzanne Lenglen, the French player who dominated the women's game between 1914 and 1926—she was nicknamed La Divine—drank brandy and cried during matches. Jimmy Connors made lewd gestures at fans. John McEnroe shouted at officials. "I shouldn't be playing tennis now," he told the *Times* after a loss in 1986. "I'm letting things affect me and I'm embarrassed." He left the tour for six months.

Racquet smashing is the most common means of catharsis. Goran Ivanisevic had to default a 2000 match because he had broken all his racquets. In 2008, Mikhail Youzhny hit himself in the forehead with his racquet so hard that it left a bloody gash. Marat Safin, a two-time slam winner, who was as tormented as he was gifted, has estimated that he smashed seven hundred racquets in his career. He's said to have played with shards of graphite embedded in his arm.

Almost every player smashes racquets, and all of them rant and mutter. "Tennis is the sport in which you talk to yourself. No athletes talk to themselves like tennis players," Agassi wrote in his autobiography, *Open*. "Why? Because tennis is so damned lonely. Only boxers can understand the loneliness of tennis players—and yet boxers have their corner men and managers." And, during a match, unlike boxers, tennis players can't talk to or touch even their opponents, let alone a coach.

Andy Murray, the No. 1 men's player, can keep up a monologue on the court for hours. He has become a mentor to Kyrgios, and FaceTimes with him regularly. "I've experienced a lot of what he is going through," Murray wrote in an email. "As athletes, we're supposed to be mentally strong, and if you are seen to be talking about feelings or anything like that, not believing in yourself or backing yourself or struggling to cope with pressure, that's seen as a negative." He went on, "But there is also a lot of pressure and it's not always that easy to deal with everything."

Still, Kyrgios is not like Murray, who is one of the hardest workers on tour. Murray recently invited Kyrgios to join him for a training period. "That was a quick no for me, because I know he's going to be training four, five hours a day," Kyrgios said. "We were probably going to have to be doing these protein shakes." Kyrgios is also not like McEnroe, who could never turn off his competitive instincts, or Agassi, though he comes closest to sounding like him. "When he was in it, Andre had amazing practice habits," Gilbert, his former coach, told me. "He was a hard worker. Those are things you hear that Nick struggles with a little bit. Andre would have a patch where he wasn't as committed, but when he was committed he put in the time—unbelievable—on the practice court."

In January, at the Australian Open, Agassi gave a rare press conference, in which he talked about Kyrgios. Three days earlier, Kyrgios had crashed in the second round, after being up two sets to love against the unassuming Andreas Seppi. Thousands of people, in his native country, had booed Kyrgios off the court. Agassi cautioned against vilifying Kyrgios. "I do share your feelings that in watching him it feels, at first glance, very offensive to see so much talent, to see somebody in the sport that means a great deal to so many, sort of disregarded," Agassi said. "But, with that being said, the journey I lived has taught me a lot about how deep one's struggles can be and how much good can still exist at the same time. I don't know his background. I know that I was always somebody that cared more than I portrayed, because it was my defense. It was my way of hiding myself from myself."

After the Australian Open, Kyrgios was in a "dark place." He went to Miami to be with his girlfriend, the Australian player Ajla Tomljanović, whom he's been dating for two years. He thought about taking a break from tennis; he didn't know for how long. But then he got a call from

Lleyton Hewitt, a former champion who is now the captain of Australia's Davis Cup team, urging him to play in the tournament. Top players rarely participate. But for Kyrgios it was a lifeline. "It was the best thing I could have done," he said.

The other players were apprehensive about Kyrgios's state of mind, but when he arrived in Melbourne, he was fully committed. He led the practice sessions with intensity; he was the first to start picking up balls. He spent extra time hitting with the youngest player. He embraced being part of a team. In February, the Australians defeated the Czech Republic. Two months later, they beat a strong American squad, with Kyrgios defeating Sam Querrey, a lanky big server, to clinch the tie. Afterward, Kyrgios lifted up Hewitt and carried him down to the court, before being engulfed by his teammates. "I love being on the bench, supporting someone else," he said later. "I just love that you win together, you take a loss together."

That match capped a remarkable run for Kyrgios. Between the two Davis Cup rounds, he beat Djokovic twice, and Zverev twice, and played Federer to nearly a draw in the semifinals of the Miami Open. It was a three-set, three-tiebreak affair in which the intensity never dropped. Brad Gilbert, who was courtside, told me that he considered it the highest-quality match this year. What really struck Gilbert, though, was how hard the crowd rooted against Kyrgios. They hissed; they tried to rattle him; they called balls out in the middle of points. For the most part, Kyrgios kept his cool. Then, on the last point, he pulverized his racquet. He was devastated to lose.

"I felt like I was pretty much unbeatable during that time," Kyrgios told me. "I don't know if I had a mind-set that this is what I want to be doing right now. I didn't have a choice. But I felt like I had one goal, and that was to compete every day." He seemed to be settling into his talent. In May, he announced that he had started working with a coach, Sébastien Grosjean, a French former player who lives in Boca Raton, where Tomljanović trains. "It's a challenge, a big one," Grosjean told me. He has been trying to persuade Kyrgios to get a fitness coach, to prevent injuries and to help him build up his body for the marathons of the slams. "He can be a better athlete. But it's new for him. It has to come from him." Grosjean sounded like Kyrgios. "He has to understand," he added.

After his wins this spring, Kyrgios was on the short list of dark horses at the French Open. But, when he talked about his recent success, he didn't first point to his results. He spoke about getting to spend a month with Tomljanović, having a single goal each day, and being part of the Davis Cup team.

The tour moved from hard courts to clay, which blunts Kyrgios's power and makes him run. After his grandfather died, in May, he skipped a tournament in Estoril, Portugal, and flew back to Australia for a week. He picked up a racquet for only twenty minutes; when the time came to head to the next tournament, in Madrid, he told his family that he didn't want to go. As soon as he arrived in Europe, homesickness set in.

His body wasn't ready. He reinjured his hip and lost a desultory match to Nadal. He pulled out of Rome, lost in Lyon, and then lost in the second round of the French Open, to Kevin Anderson, a strong player but one Kyrgios should have beaten. He wrecked two racquets during the match and asked someone in the crowd for a beer. "Honest to God, get me one now," he begged.

"You're kidding," the spectator responded.

"I don't think so," Kyrgios said.

He was later criticized for having played doubles the day before, when he and his countryman Jordan Thompson upset the No. 2 seeds, instead of saving his energy for singles. But he intends to play more doubles, not less. It removes the pressure of being alone on the court, he told me, and reminds him that tennis "can be fun."

He arrived in London two weeks before the start of Wimbledon and rented a house. His mother and Tomljanović joined him, and his mom cooked; it felt a little like home. On June 19th, he played his first match of the grass-court season, in the Aegon International, at the Queen's Club. Practicing, he looked relaxed. He has liked grass since he first played on it as a kid, at a tournament in Australia. It helps his big serve skid, and it suits his aggressive style.

At Queen's, Kyrgios faced the American Donald Young in the first round. They were on serve halfway through the first set when Kyrgios's right foot slipped on the newly laid grass; his left knee buckled unnaturally, and he went down, rolling over in pain. He had strained his hip again. Kyrgios limped through the rest of the set, which he lost in a tie-break, and then retired from the tournament.

Still, he vowed to play Wimbledon. He thinks he can win. And if he doesn't—not now, not ever? Kyrgios has said that he would like to emulate the career of Gaël Monfils, a Frenchman known for his leaping shots and questionable strategies, and for being one of the most talented players never to win a major. When I mentioned Monfils's unfulfilled promise, Kyrgios challenged me. "He's got to, I think, eight in the world," he said. "He's won a lot of tournaments. He's been to semifinals of grand slams. He's made a ton of money. He's probably one of the happiest guys on tour." He added, "Ultimately, he's just a guy who wants people to enjoy watching tennis."

Kyrgios sometimes elicits comparisons to Monfils, if only because they both have a propensity for tweeners. But Kyrgios doesn't have the same carefree demeanor on the court. "I think he struggles with who he wants to be and who he is," Rennae Stubbs, an Australian commentator and former player, told me. The question in the tennis world tends to be whether Kyrgios will figure out how to win consistently. But for Kyrgios maybe there's a different project. "I just would like to be happy," he said. "That's a tough one for me."

This piece was originally published in the July 10 and 17, 2017, issue of The New Yorker.

Tomato Can Blues

MARY PILON

Scott DiPonio raced to make sure everything was in order—the fighters were ready, the ring girls were on time and the Bud Light was cold.

DiPonio was a local promoter who organized amateur cage fights that looked more like barroom brawls than glitzy Las Vegas bouts. With a mix of grit, sweat and blood, the fights had caught on in rural Michigan, and DiPonio's Feb. 2 event, called Caged Aggression, drew hundreds of fans, even with cage-side seats going for $35.

Charlie Rowan, an undistinguished heavyweight, was scheduled to fight that night at Streeters, a dank nightclub that hosted cage fights in Traverse City.

Rowan's cage name was Freight Train, but he was more like a caboose—plodding and slow, a bruiser whose job was to fill out the ring and get knocked down.

He was what the boxing world used to call a "tomato

can." The term's origins are unclear, but perhaps it's as simple as this: knock a tomato can over, and red stuff spills out.

Rowan certainly wasn't in it for the money. He was an amateur who loved fighting so much he did it for free.

An hour before the Caged Aggression fights began, DiPonio's cellphone rang. It was Rowan's girlfriend, so frantic she could hardly get the words out, DiPonio said. He asked her to take a deep breath, and, on the verge of tears, she told him that Rowan had crashed his car. He was being airlifted to a hospital. It didn't look good.

Two days later, DiPonio said, she called back. Rowan, only twenty-five years old, was dead.

DiPonio drove for two hours from Traverse City to Gladwin for a makeshift memorial at the home of Rowan's girlfriend. Rowan's mother sat in the living room, quietly weeping.

DiPonio and other promoters planned a string of benefits for the Rowan family, including one called the Fight for Charlie. The fighters were enemies in the cage, but they pulled together to help one of their own. A heavyweight who had once knocked out Rowan in under ninety seconds agreed to work as a judge at the largest benefit.

The Fight for Charlie took place on March 9. Ring girls sold raffle tickets to a crowd of about a thousand. A young fighter declared from the cage that he was dedicating his bout to Rowan's memory.

"Thank you for helping us raise money for Charlie Rowan's family," a promoter wrote on Facebook after one of the benefits. "Thank you for letting it all out in the cage for us."

He added that Rowan was "there with us in spirit and would have been very proud of all of you!"

Less than two weeks later, a Gladwin gun store was robbed.

When Scott DiPonio, the fight promoter, saw the suspect's mug shot on the next day's news, his stomach dropped. It was the late Charlie Rowan, back from the dead.

A Blood-Soaked Allure

Mixed martial arts was born as a seedy sport on the fringes of society. The matches were short, loud and brutal, fights for those who found boxing too tame. Over the years, it's grown into a mainstream spectacle that now draws millions of viewers on television.

The sport blends techniques from jiu jitsu, kickboxing, karate, taekwondo, judo and wrestling. Certain moves, like eye gouging and shots to the crotch, are generally not allowed. Across America, kids squabbling in their backyards now dream of making it to the Ultimate Fighting Championship, just as playground basketball players picture themselves in the N.B.A.

But far from the bright lights of professional matches, shadow fighting circuits have sprung up around the country, in small towns like Kingston, Wash., and big cities like New York. It's like the early days of boxing, but with more kicks to the face.

"It's amazing that guys will get beat up for free," Christos

Piliafas, a top fighter in Michigan, said. "They just love to fight."

In Michigan, the bouts take place in nightclubs, community centers and casinos. Most are unregulated, with few safety requirements to speak of. In April, a thirty-five-year-old died after losing a fight in Port Huron.

The crude violence and underground feel of cage fighting draw lusty cheers across the state. These are not carefully negotiated bouts between millionaires trailing personal nutritionists and publicists. Inside the cage at Streeters, unknown Michigan men—factory workers, fathers, soldiers and convicts—become the Wolverine, the Bloodbath, the Spider Monkey and the Nightmare.

"You build a brotherhood," said Justin Martinson, a fighter and former Marine. "It's the closest thing to combat."

When Rowan entered the cage for the first time, he felt electric. Part of it was the cocaine—he was high, as he was for most of his fights. But he also loved the atmosphere: the chain link walls, the heavy metal music, the screaming fans.

Rowan could take a punch, but he was out of shape and showed little promise. "He was a horrible fighter," said Piliafas, who competes professionally. "He just showed up and would fight. He was a great first fight for someone."

Rowan kept his brown hair cut close and wore a thin mustache. He had a tattoo of a Viking on his left shoulder, the Grim Reaper on his right; Jesus' face on his right leg; and MOM on his left wrist. His newest tattoo was a gothic D inside a diamond, the logo for DiPonio's mixed martial arts team. To Rowan, the Diamond D fighters were family, even if they didn't know what to make of him.

Rowan had struggled to find meaningful work since dropping out of school before tenth grade. He spent time in telemarketing and pipeline installation. He even worked on the carnival circuit assembling rides. He fathered three children with three women, but he drifted from all of them.

Rowan's real family admired his passion for the cage. "I thought maybe it would be good for him," his mother, Lynn Gardner, said. "He seemed to like it, and I thought finally he found something and can take out his aggression. Maybe it could help him turn his life around."

Rowan was from Gladwin, a city of 3,000 that's barely a blip amid Central Michigan's endless wheat, corn, and soybean farms. His story was pieced together from more than fifty interviews with relatives, local fighters, and Michigan law enforcement officials, as well as from police reports, court records, and family letters.

Gladwin families hunt on weekends, and the town's quiet roads include Deer, Elk, and Antler Streets. It takes five minutes to drive across town, from McDonald's to the west to Shopko to the east. Jobs are hard to come by. Slouching houses with plywood-covered windows are as common as stop signs.

In some ways, Rowan had been preparing for the cage his whole life. His father, also named Charles, had beaten him and his brother ever since they were little.

"His dad would put him on the floor and stomp him in

the head," his mother said. "When he couldn't take it out on Chuckie, he would take it out on me."

Home was cigarettes, beer, and the blare of a television over his parents' constant arguments. The family moved around Michigan as Rowan's father picked up and lost factory jobs. For a while, the family gathered soda bottles for spare change.

"I thought about leaving a lot," his mother said. "But I was never confident enough in myself and my abilities."

Rowan's father died of cancer in 2001. "He told Chuck that he would rather it was him"—his son—"that was dying," she said.

Even as a kid, Rowan was always in trouble. He stole from neighbors and relatives—"guns, dumb things, work tools, money," Scott Gardner, his stepfather, said.

In the years after his father's death, Rowan was arrested on charges of marijuana distribution and failure to pay child support. He was charged with criminal sexual misconduct as a teenager and failure to register as a sex offender in 2007. Those records are sealed under state law. Rowan spent most of 2012 in jail on check fraud charges.

During those years, he used cocaine and did some work for drug dealers, but he kept that a secret from his family.

Through mutual acquaintances, he met Michael A. Gomez, a convict with drug and weapons charges dating back at least twenty years. The sheriff's office knew Gomez had ties to the Latin Kings and the Mexican Mafia Gang.

While Rowan was ferrying drugs in Three Rivers in 2010, before he began cage fighting, he claimed to have lost Gomez's shipment, maybe worth as much as $80,000. As Rowan told it, a group of thieves jumped him, cracked his ribs, and stole the drugs.

Now, Rowan owed money to impatient people. He tried to lie low, but in January, a group of men beat him up behind Shopko, leaving him with two black eyes, broken ribs, and blood on his baseball cap, he told friends at the time.

Rowan was desperate. Then, while he was watching TV at his girlfriend's house, a show caught his attention. It was on the Investigation Discovery channel, something about a guy who staged his own death so he could start his life anew.

A Way Out

Rowan had felt as if he were drowning for a while now. He owed money to drug dealers. He couldn't keep a job. His hobby was getting beaten up in public. Now this fake-death scheme landed like a life preserver.

If people thought he was dead, he and his girlfriend, Rosa Martinez, could move far from Michigan. Maybe New Mexico. They could begin again.

"I wanted a fresh start," he said in one of a series of interviews conducted both in person and over the phone. "To pick up and start someplace new where no one knew us."

The phone calls were the first step—Rowan said he was

there when Martinez called DiPonio, the fight promoter, to announce the car crash. She later called his mother. Rowan said it broke his heart to think of his mother picturing him dead, but he saw no other way. He could hear Martinez as she made the calls, and he said that first step of the hoax "almost killed me."

When Martinez called back two days later to say Rowan was dead, he said, he choked up and had to leave the room.

The mourners gathered at Martinez's home to remember Charles H. Rowan, father, son, friend, and cage fighter. The guests walked up a wooden ramp leading to the front door, past a sprinkling of cigarette butts that dotted the yard's patchy snow.

Inside the small living room, lined with brown carpet and wood-paneled walls, sat two young children, along with Rowan's mother, who was sobbing.

Martinez looked grief-stricken. She brushed off questions about funeral arrangements and other practical matters, making clear she was not yet ready.

As the group sat quietly in the living room, she stepped away to collect a bag that she said had been retrieved from the accident.

She pulled out a white baseball cap that was stained with blood. A young boy began to cry.

They mourned Rowan as a lost soul gone too soon. But he had not gone anywhere. Rowan was upstairs throughout the memorial, he said, hiding in a child's bedroom until the guests left. While his mother cried and his girlfriend accepted condolences, Rowan worked hard not to make a sound.

He said he thought about walking downstairs to interrupt the grieving, ending the ruse right there.

From upstairs, he said, he could hear the sobs coming from the living room, sounds that took him by surprise. "For people to care about me," he said, "it meant something."

But now, he needed to play dead, which meant he needed to block all that out. He looked out the bedroom's small window, past the lawn and out toward the Rite Aid. He tried not to break his gaze.

Trapped

If this was the afterlife, Rowan didn't much care for it.

He spent most of the next six weeks hiding out in his girlfriend's home, watching TV and working out in a small makeshift gym. He said he closed his bank account and disabled his Facebook page. He made late-night trips to Rite Aid and even kept Martinez company for a meeting at her children's school. The couple said they were possibly moving to New Mexico, a school official later told the police.

"I went stir crazy," Rowan said. "I couldn't call any of my friends; I couldn't go anywhere. I love Rosa more than life itself, but it's just too much to be around the same person all of the time."

Despite his efforts, the hoax began to fray. Skeptics took

to Facebook, where they peppered the fight promoters with questions about death certificates and obituaries.

The promoters took offense. "I said: 'How dare you question this? The dude is dead! Have some respect,'" the promoter Joe Shaw said.

Rowan's family wanted to know what happened to his body. Scott Gardner, his stepfather, called local hospitals but didn't find anyone who could help. "We felt like we didn't have any facts," Gardner said. Sympathy cards began to arrive, some of them with checks included, but the family set them aside.

Rumors about Rowan were bound to reach the people he owed money, and by mid-March, they apparently had. While his loved ones still thought he was dead, he sneaked away to meet with Michael Gomez in Gladwin—the circumstances remain murky. Gomez and his lawyer did not respond to multiple requests for comment.

At the meeting, Gomez threatened to hurt Martinez and her kids, Rowan said.

The walls were closing in. But Charlie Rowan, still presumed dead, had one last idea.

An Opportunity to Strike

On a cold March afternoon, Roxie Robinette served lunch to her husband, Richard. The bell rang next door in their store, Guns & Stuff: a new customer.

Richard got up, leaving Roxie behind to fold laundry in front of the TV.

Guns & Stuff was a mom-and-pop shop that sold revolvers, pistols, and shotguns, along with hunting jackets and Skittles. Mounted buck heads eyed customers from the wall. A sign read, "No Pissy Attitudes."

The gun store played the role a diner might in another town—the place where neighbors gossip about the weather and one another. All of Gladwin knew Richard Robinette, a retired plumber and banjo player who'd been in poor health. Even Rowan knew Robinette: he had recently sold Robinette a rifle he stole from a relative, Rowan said.

On the afternoon of March 18, the sheriff said, Michael Bowman drove Rowan and his girlfriend to the store in a maroon Chevrolet Blazer. Bowman was among Rowan's closest friends, a lanky, baby-faced man in his early twenties with a criminal history of his own. A lawyer for Martinez did not respond to multiple requests for interviews. Bowman's lawyer declined to comment.

Rowan sat in the back seat, wearing a trench coat and sneakers. He smeared black dollar-store makeup around his eyes and tied a red bandanna around his mouth. The finishing touch was a Batman mask he said he took from his girlfriend's son.

Rowan was going to rob Guns & Stuff—"hit a lick" was his term. His girlfriend would be the decoy.

The police said she walked into the store first, carrying

an iPhone in her pocket that was on an open call to Rowan, waiting down the road. That way, he could listen in and find the right moment to strike.

After a few minutes, Rowan got out of the car and headed toward the neon "OPEN" sign. But on the way, he realized he made a mistake: he forgot the weapon, a pink canister of pepper spray. He had left it in the car.

He was carrying a hammer from his toolbox—he was going to use it to break into the cases holding the guns. But now, the hammer would take on a starring role.

He pushed open the door and swung the hammer at Robinette's head, knocking him from his stool. Rowan later said he had been aiming for Robinette's shoulder and missed.

The blow opened up the side of Robinette's head, spilling a pool of blood. The sheriff's report called the wound a "jagged hole approximately the size of a quarter, which appeared to go through his skull." The blood stain soaking the carpet was, a county detective wrote, the "size of a dinner plate."

Even Rowan was shaken. "There was a lot of blood," he said. "Enough to scare me. I'm a man used to seeing a lot of blood, but that was a lot of blood."

Rowan kicked his girlfriend in the arm, hoping to make her seem like a second victim. He shoved eight handguns into his red and black duffel bag and then, on his way out, noticed Robinette's wallet sticking out of his pocket. He grabbed that, too, and tore off through the woods, toward a church parking lot where Bowman was waiting.

In the car, the two hardly spoke.

"I was in shock with what had just happened," Rowan said. "I thought I had just killed somebody."

Martinez kept to her part of the plan and called 911 from Guns & Stuff. Within minutes, Detective Sgt. James Cuddie and Officer Eric Killian were en route. They stopped a hundred yards from the store, on the shoulder of the road, to put on bulletproof vests.

They approached on foot, and inside found Rowan's girlfriend cowered in the back. Robinette sat on a stool, holding the left side of his head. Cuddie asked him what happened, and he replied slowly, "I don't know, Jim."

Cuddie then turned to interview Martinez. She hadn't herself been in trouble before, but her social circle sometimes overlapped with Cuddie's investigations. Martinez told him she had been there to sell some of her family's guns when a masked robber burst through the door.

Meanwhile, Bowman later told the police, he and Rowan drove toward a vacant home where the mother of Rowan's girlfriend had recently lived.

Rowan stashed the robbery evidence around the house—two pistols in the dining room vent, the duffel bag behind the refrigerator, the sneakers in the garage attic. He stuffed the Batman mask above the kitchen sink, still filled with dirty dishes and an empty bottle of Diet Pepsi Wild Cherry.

Rowan paced the house, waiting for news, waiting for his girlfriend. He smoked an entire pack of Newports.

Finally, Rowan called the phone his girlfriend had carried during the robbery. Cuddie answered and identified himself as Jim. He asked who was calling. Rowan, flustered, gave his cousin's name.

He could tell that Cuddie was suspicious. The life preserver had begun to feel like a noose.

Connecting the Pieces

With a thick mustache, his hair cut short, and a no-nonsense demeanor, James Cuddie would have a hard time passing as anything other than a cop. Not that he would try—everyone in Gladwin County knew him as Jim, the county detective, including many of the people he arrested. Sometimes, as Cuddie eased suspects into the back of his police car, they apologized to him by name.

It didn't take long for Cuddie and his colleagues to connect Rowan with the Guns & Stuff robbery. When officers dropped off Martinez, they saw his ID in her home.

Then Bowman visited the sheriff's office and said that Rowan may have been involved in the robbery. That was also a roundabout way of saying that Rowan might not be quite as dead as people had thought.

For weeks, Cuddie had heard rumors about Rowan's death, but he didn't think much about them one way or the other. "I didn't know it to be true or untrue," he said. "At that point it wasn't an issue. I'm working on other cases."

But now, with Richard Robinette in intensive care, Cuddie's interest was piqued.

It should have been the most straightforward of questions: is Charlie Rowan dead or alive? But it had become bizarrely muddled.

The day after the robbery, Cuddie called the Saginaw County medical examiner's office, which housed records for the county's deceased. Officials there confirmed that there was no death certificate for Charles Howard Rowan. The medical examiner declared it "unlikely" that Rowan had died.

That was enough for Cuddie to surmise that Rowan was out there on the run. "Rowan and Martinez were people of interest that needed to be located," he wrote in his report.

On March 19, the sheriff's office released Rowan's mug shot to the local news media.

Big John Yeubanks, a fight promoter, was smoking a cigarette in his home office, half-listening to the TV news. The story of the day was a robbery of Guns & Stuff.

The suspect's mug shot flashed across the screen, and Yeubanks snapped to attention.

There was no mistaking it, yet it could not be.

"I know that guy!" he shouted. "He's not supposed to be alive!"

Yeubanks called the sheriff to say there must have been a mistake—they were looking for a dead man.

Word quickly spread through the cage fighting world. DiPonio's girlfriend pulled up the mug shot on her phone. Goatee, square jaw, pursed lips—it was Charlie Rowan.

"She showed it to me," DiPonio said, "and I nearly threw up right there."

At the Gladwin County Sheriff's Office, the phone had been ringing steadily since the mug shots were released. The officers kept hearing the same strange thing: the suspect, Charlie Rowan, was already dead.

Weeks later, sitting in his cluttered basement office, Cuddie laughed at the deluge of calls. He described the one he received from DiPonio, so sure that Rowan was dead.

"I told him that I had reason to believe," Cuddie said, "that Mr. Rowan was very much alive."

Voice from the Beyond

Rowan's vision of starting a new life, in New Mexico or anywhere else, was turning to dust.

He and his girlfriend were hiding out from the local police, from federal agents working the case, from the people Rowan owed money, and from the fight promoters he tricked.

The Guns & Stuff robbery and the manhunt had put the town on edge. Rowan's mother, still grieving for her son, was at the Chappel Dam Grocery when she heard about the attack. "I thought, 'At least I know my son didn't do it,'" she said.

Her relief wouldn't last long. Soon, her phone rang. It was her son, Charlie, no longer dead.

For six weeks, she thought she'd lost him, at age twenty-five.

She never said goodbye. Now, here he was, on the phone. He had one question for her: could she give him a ride?

His mother drove in a fog, past the familiar barns, churches and homes that lined the road. Finally, on the right, she saw her son, waving his arms to flag her down.

Still confused, she asked where he'd been for so long. This was all a lie? They both started crying. Rowan mumbled something about being "out of state." He got out of the car at his girlfriend's home, the same place his mother had cried during his memorial the month before.

His mother went to the sheriff's office in tears the next day to tell Cuddie that her son was indeed alive. She said she was afraid he'd robbed Guns & Stuff and hit old man Robinette.

That night, Rowan said, he went to Saginaw, where he gave Gomez six of the stolen guns to pay down his debt, worth $1,000 per handgun. Gomez later told the authorities that he bought only one pistol from Rowan, according to a police report. Gomez was arrested soon after on charges of possessing weapons as a felon.

Rowan and his girlfriend were still hiding out. They booked a room at the Knights Inn in Saginaw, where a bed cost $50. "I was on edge all night, me and Rosa," Rowan said. "I knew I was fighting a losing battle."

They stayed on the run for about forty-eight hours, moving from one spot to another. The scrambling didn't throw off Cuddie and his colleagues.

On March 20, two days after the robbery, they tracked

Rowan and his girlfriend to a friend's apartment in Unionville. The couple were arrested at about 7:15 A.M.

It was all over—and Cuddie had a definitive answer. Charlie Rowan was not dead. But he would be going away for a long, long time.

He told Cuddie that he didn't mean for it to happen this way. He walked the officers through the robbery and told them where they could find the guns, the Batman mask, the stolen wallet.

The news was out. A front-page headline in the *Traverse City Record-Eagle* read, "Fighter Accused of Faking Death."

The cage fighters felt betrayed, furious that Rowan had sullied their sport's name.

"He's lucky the cops got him before the fighters did," Big John Yeubanks, the promoter, said. Organizers of the Fight for Charlie recently filed a police report in Traverse City accusing Rowan of fraud.

After the hoax was exposed, the cage fighting promoters decided to hold another benefit, this time to raise money for the Robinettes, the owners of Guns & Stuff. They have collected more than $15,000.

"We got sick of hearing about Charles Rowan and we thought, What about the Robinettes?" Yeubanks said. "Everybody was looking at this guy like he was an MMA fighter from Michigan, but in fact he was a small-time tough guy who got in a cage a couple of times."

Today, Richard Robinette is back home after a recovery that's surprised even his family and his doctors. He started playing his banjo again. He recently fixed the bathroom sink.

He doesn't remember much of the robbery, but he showed off a horseshoe of stitches on the left side of his head.

"You can't sit and cry about it," he said. "They thought I was going to die."

A few miles away, Rowan sits inside another cage, in the Gladwin County Jail. He pleaded guilty last month to armed robbery. He'll be sentenced in October.

In jail, Rowan wrote letters to his mother, trying to atone. "I did not mean to hurt that man and his family," one letter read. "I hope to see you at my visit."

Rowan's mother usually comes to see him once a week. On a recent afternoon, the two put their hands against the clear divider that separated them.

"I'm sorry you did this, too," his mother said. Rowan, wearing an orange jumpsuit, told her he figured he'd be locked up for the rest of her life.

He reads mysteries in jail. During his first few weeks behind bars, he tried to catch glimpses of his girlfriend, who was being held nearby. She recently pleaded guilty to armed robbery charges.

He goes over the whole strange story, step by step. He finds himself returning to the fake memorial, and the sounds of people sobbing for him.

"I didn't realize how I impacted other people's lives," he

said. "I don't hold myself in high regard. I'm not a good person, I'm not a good dad, and most of the time I'm not a good son."

He thinks about his girlfriend, Rosa, and wonders whether they'll ever be together again.

"It's like . . ." He struggled to get the words out. "It's like we just died."

This piece was originally published in the New York Times *on September 18, 2013.*

Washington Generals Win!

MATT NISSENBAUM

"Let me get this straight. You took all the money you made franchising your name, and bet it *against* the Harlem Globetrotters?!"

"I thought the Generals were due!"

—KRUSTY THE CLOWN AND HIS ACCOUNTANT,

"Homie the Clown," *The Simpsons*, season 6, episode 15

It has happened before. Buster Douglas, a relatively untested and unknown boxer, knocked out then-undefeated and undisputed champion Mike Tyson in the tenth round of their 1990 title bout, as a 42–1 underdog. Trailing the Atlanta Braves by four and a half games for the wild card spot with fifteen games left in the regular season, the 2011 St. Louis Cardinals were 999–1 dogs who went on to win the World Series. Perennial relegation candidates Leicester City won the Premier League championship in 2015 despite starting the season at odds of 5,000–1. But, alas for Krusty and his investment, the Washington Generals maintained their reputation as lovable losers that day, taking the L once again to their perma-rivals, the Harlem Globetrotters.

The brainchild of former professional basketball player Louis "Red" Klotz and Harlem Globetrotters owner Abe Saperstein, the Generals' job was literally to lose, game after game after game. In the time since their founding, they have done their jobs so well that their name has become synonymous with getting beaten. This may be best shown through Krusty's degenerate bet on the Generals to win, with which the writers of *The Simpsons* went out on a limb that the general viewing public would understand the joke—and they did.

Since their introduction in 1952 the Generals (and their numerous aliases, such as the Atlantic City Seagulls, the New York Nationals, International Elite, and the World All-Stars) have weathered over sixteen thousand losses at the hands of the kings of basketball comedy. Sixteen thousand! That's not a typo. It's easy to think, given those results, that the Generals have had a lineup no better than the guys from a local pickup game at the gym, but that's actually not the case. The Generals were (and are) composed of legit basketball contenders, made up of former collegiate journeymen and international spectacles, such as seven-foot-seven Paul "Tiny" Sturgess. Of course, the Generals losses typically stemmed from gags they just couldn't defend, like getting their shorts pulled down midcourt, defending dunks taken from ladders, or having baskets scored against them suddenly worth more than the standard two or three points, as opposed to their own incompetence. Despite their actual talent and competitive spirit, they were resigned to be nothing more than the perennial fall guys.

But outside of the staged shenanigans, both the Generals and the Globetrotters were actually good. Really good, in fact. The Globetrotters' starting lineup has demolished both college and national teams in exhibition games, including a lopsided win against the then-defending national champions Syracuse in 2004, while the Generals have defeated the Taiwanese national team and an Army team. But this was the point—the Generals had to be good when no one was fooling around, in order to establish themselves as worthwhile contenders.

The best example of the Generals' actual prowess is a notable accident on January 5, 1971, when the biggest losers in history accidentally beat the mighty Globetrotters, 100–99.

Accounts of that game have differed over the years, but the general story is the same. The Globetrotters' top player at the time, Curly Neal, was out for the game, and they kept missing some of their planned theatrical drives to the hoop. The Generals, meanwhile, were hitting shots at a freakish clip. As is customary for a Globetrotters game, no one was really paying attention to the score, until just a few minutes were left and the Generals were up by twelve.

Instead of reverting to gags that the Generals couldn't defend, the Harlem Globetrotters decided to play for real, to earn the win the hard way. A flurry of offense forced overtime, led by the heroics of standout player Meadowlark Lemon, but a last-second miss by Lemon combined with the inability of the "referees" to stop the clock, put the win in the hands of Red Klotz and the Washington Generals. The rare exhilaration of winning spilled over to the locker room, where the Generals showered themselves in shaken cans of orange soda, since champagne was impossible to come by in the dry town of Martin, Tennessee, where the infamous game took place.

In recent years, the Generals have actually tried to pivot the public perception that they can't ball with the big boys. In 2017, the Generals brought on TV analyst and former NBA standout Kenny Smith as general manager and former NBA player and experienced manager Sam Worthen as coach. They held an ironic "draft" to pick up new talent, including basketball dad extraordinaire LaVar Ball and MMA fighter Conor McGregor. Led by former NBA journeyman Sundiata Gaines, among others, the Generals even entered a team in ESPN's The Basketball Tournament, a 5-on-5, winner-take-all tournament where the winners took home a $2 million cash prize. In true Generals fashion, despite the rare opportunity to play serious, competitive basketball, they were knocked out in the first round.

Never ones to let their spirits be dashed, the Washington Generals know they are always one game away from beating the most prolific winners in sports history. And just like Krusty, I hope they're due.

The Guy Wearing a Hat: Dick Beardsley and the Biggest Second-Place Finishes in Marathon History

ANDREW LEHREN

The start of the 1982 Boston Marathon was too hot—already 70 degrees at noon. The men wore white socks as if they were a requirement, pulled up over their ankles. The shorts were cut awkwardly. Shoe companies had not yet deemed it worth their while to splash their logos across the singlets of every top-ranked runner. The few who got sponsorships usually received just a tiny stipend.

If this were a movie, the leading man would be the favorite, Alberto Salazar. Born in Cuba but raised in Boston, Salazar played the local hero, a dark-haired, handsome star burning with ambition. His victory the past fall in New York set a new world record and earned his spot as the leader of the next generation of American runners. This was long before his fall as head coach of Nike's now-defunct Oregon

Project. In 2019, Salazar received a four-year ban for doping offenses and a separate temporary suspension in the following year as an investigation procedes for verbal abuse of his athletes. He contested both allegations.

The supporting cast at the Boston starting line would include the boyish four-time winner Bill Rodgers, no longer fast enough to be the favorite, but smart enough to make anyone anxious that he could make them pay for a mistake.

But in the black-and-white photos of the early crowd of leaders, one other runner stands out. As if some ham-fisted movie director was trying to draw our attention to him among the bobbing heads coursing downward out of Hopkinton in the opening miles: the guy wearing a hat.

What would unfold would be one of the most stunning second-place finishes in the history of running.

The ill-fitting white paper painter's cap sat on the head of a tall Minnesotan, Dick Beardsley, who would later begin his autobiography, *Staying the Course: A Runner's Toughest Race,* by proclaiming, "I never had designs on becoming a world-class athlete. All I wanted was a date."

Like a typical Midwest boy, he thought if he made the high school football team, it would increase his chances. The coaches found him too skinny. So he tried running. He worked his way up from junior varsity on his high school track team to college teams in Minnesota and South Dakota.

He was good enough to earn a visit to the national cross-country championships, but others were faster. With little training he tried a nearby marathon in 1977 and found it "interesting." He married a woman who worked at a bank while he peddled sneakers at a local running store.

Beardsley kept getting better, and soon was good enough that New Balance covered his travel expenses. More important, they teamed him with Rodgers's coach, Bill Squires. The modest encouragement from New Balance meant so much to Beardsley that the night before the Boston marathon, he turned down a more lucrative offer to switch to Adidas.

By mile 17, in the Newton hills, it was two-man race. Salazar, of course, was there, thrilling the hometown fans. But the leader was Beardsley. The two did not need to turn to see where the other was—they could just look down at the shadows cast from the sun. The course funneled to narrow chutes as spectators bunched in to cheer the leaders. There was no crowd control; more like the chaos that cyclists face going up the mountains the Tour de France.

Boston police motorcycles buzzed around the leaders to clear a path. The leaders were hurting but did not want to show the pain. Beardsley later recalled he could no longer feel his legs for the last five miles.

He tried surging in speed to shake Salazar. Near the top of Heartbreak Hill, at mile 21, Beardsley went over to a wheelchair athlete and cheered him on, partly with genuine encouragement, and partly hoping Salazar would witness his apparent ease and start breaking mentally. The tactic did not work. Neither was giving up.

Then came the downhills into Boston. Beardsley had

come up with a homemade preparation for this part of the course: he drummed on his thighs hundreds of times a day, believing it would toughen his quads for the pounding they were about to take.

The two runners never separated. Beardsley, the brim of his painter's hat now pushed backward to fend off the burning sun behind their backs, was barely first.

But with only a mile to go, Salazar cut to the front. Beardsley, though he was close behind, knew his opportunity was fading. Salazar had a strong kick. Beardsley could not accelerate like that. And he knew it.

Then came the moment of controversy, one that runners still debate. Today, it seems inconceivable that it could even have happened, with the professional choreography of major marathons. There are no barricades. Crowds on the street leave the runners little room to maneuver. A small but growing gap now separates Beardsley from Salazar. They bank a turn. Beardsley begins to regain some of the lost ground.

But one of the half-dozen escorting police motorcyclists suddenly cuts in front of Beardsley, wrongly believing the runner is fading. Beardsley is forced to hesitate a moment and swing outside. The longer way to catch up to Salazar.

He somehow still narrows the distance, but the finish line looms. Only two seconds separate the pair. But there is not enough marathon left, and those couple seconds translate into several strides that look like an eternity.

If the motorcyclist had not cut in front of Beardsley,

would it have mattered? Beardsley discounts the possibility, saying that he expended all he had on the course and Salazar had the better day. But in a marathon that came down to moments, there is an uncertainty. If he had edged closer sooner, the dynamics of the race could have changed.

All Beardsley knows is that the two brought out the best in each other.

"If Alberto was not in that race, there is no way I would have run 2:08," Beardsley said. "And if you spoke with Alberto, I'm sure he'd say the same thing."

Beardsley's second place was the second-fastest marathon ever run in the world. And for more than a decade, Beardsley's time stood as the fastest ever clocked by someone born in the United States.

More than thirty-five years later, Beardsley's effort remains among the ten-fastest marathon times ever run by someone from the United States.

The epic race was recounted with grace by journalist John Brant in his *Duel in the Sun*, and in occasional talks reliving the race.

The iconic moment, though, is not Beardsley's swerve. It happened after the race. Salazar was on the top of the podium, collecting his trophy and crowned with a garland wreath, like an athlete from ancient Greece. Instead of a self-congratulatory fist pump, he reached over to Beardsley, on the lower part of the podium, grabbed hold of his arm and elevated it with his own.

"One of the most coveted awards in running is being up on that podium in Boston," Beardsley said. "Getting the laurel wreath on your head, that's your moment."

"For Alberto to bring me up to that stand with him, and when they were raising his arm in victory, he was raising mine right along with his, that is something I will never ever forget." he said. "That gesture shows what sportsmanship is all about.

"I still get goose bumps when I think about that."

While many marathoners are familiar with the Duel in the Sun, what is less well known about Beardsley is that this was actually the *second* time in a little over a year where he wanted to win a marathon outright and instead found himself and a rival with arms raised.

In March 1981, Beardsley flew to the first-ever London Marathon; an event, like Boston, now ranked among the world's major marathons.

Beardsley wanted his first victory. The BBC pegged him as a favorite. He thought the stiffest competitors would be hometown favorites, top British distance runners like veteran podium finisher Trevor Wright. He was wrong.

Beardsley was stiff from a bad night of sleep. His modest travel money landed him in a hotel with a bed so small that when he stretched out, his legs hung over the end.

The race began in a gentle rain. Instead of a traditional starter gun, the organizers blasted a Howitzer. Beardsley dashed from the start to be among the leaders.

For Beardsley, this was emblematic of a key shift in his

approach to racing that began a year earlier. Before, he concentrated on his times. Now he concentrated on tactics and the positions of other runners.

"I told myself, 'If you ever want to see if you can run with the big boys, you need to forget about time and go out and be competitive,'" he recalled. "I'm going out to do my best to see if I can win the darn thing."

A little over halfway, crossing the Thames over the Tower Bridge, there was no clear leader. Eight runners jostled for the lead, among them the home country favorite, Trevor Wright. Beardsley decided to quicken the pace.

"The only guy who came with me was a guy named Inge Simonsen, from Norway," Beardsley recalled. "I had no idea who he was."

They headed into the aging industrial Docklands section of the city. Few spectators lined the streets. Each runner threw surges at each other to see if he could break the other.

Nothing worked.

Beardsley worried not only about Simonsen, but about the course itself—the wet, slippery, uneven cobblestones in the late miles. "Cobblestones are sticking up, and they are like an ice rink." He recalled thinking, "I'm afraid I'm going to fall down."

In this Duel in the Rain, the two runners pressed past Big Ben and Buckingham Palace, shoulder to shoulder. "We are tailing it as hard as we can," Beardsley remembered.

They exchanged a few words. Simonsen understood a little English. In his autobiography, Beardsley wrote that just near the end, they realized they could not shake the other and agreed to cross the finish line together. Today, Beardsley said he is unsure if there ever was a spoken pact.

What he does know—and is apparent on the replay—is "we didn't even look at each other. We grabbed each other's hands and up they came."

What surprised him most was the reaction.

"The next day, the picture of him and me coming across the finish line with our arms up together was in papers all over the world," he said. "I don't think the main reason was because we were declared the winners of the first London marathon, but because it showed sportsmanship between two different countries."

Beardsley believes the winner would be largely forgotten if one or the other had finished first. Instead, with arms raised in a tie as they crossed the finish line, the image became a totem to sportsmanship.

The London Marathon has since put the image on race shirts. Both Beardsley and Simonsen have traveled back for race festivities, and the American hopes to run the marathon again in 2020.

Beardsley said he has no regrets about his running career. He knows that if he were given three more seconds, he would have won both Boston and London.

He would not trade those for the moments he had with his arm raised first with Simonsen and then Salazar.

Beardsley was not the same runner after Boston. An Achilles injury began taking its toll. He did not alter his frenetic training. He rebounded and tried one last time for the Olympics, wearing bib number 1 in the Trials to join the 1988 team. But he soon knew it was not his day. With that loss, he stepped off the world's elite marathon stage.

He looked back and thought losing Boston would be "the hardest thing in my life."

He was wrong.

Beardsley went back to work at his farm in Minnesota, but in 1989 he slipped from his tractor. His leg became entangled with the mechanism powering a corn elevator. He was spun around and desperately reached for the shut-off lever. He was able to grasp it. But his injuries were massive.

Among the lacerations and broken bones, one leg was mangled. Doctors feared one of America's greatest marathoners would face an amputation. That led to surgeries. And an addiction to pain medications. More difficulties ensued. He was running and hit by a truck. He was arrested trying to use forged prescriptions. He was divorced from his first wife and suffered business setbacks, including a bankruptcy filing.

None of that compares with the suicide of his son, Andy, on Oct. 4, 2015. He had been an army helicopter gunner in the Iraq War and would also load the wounded onto helicopters.

"I knew he had to do some things, and saw some things, that were not pleasant," Beardsley said. His son sought help from Veterans Affairs doctors in Fargo, North Dakota. He talked regularly with his father.

Still, Beardsley knew his son "would have these dark moments."

His last conversation with Andy was less than twelve hours before he killed himself.

"He said, 'Pop, I bought a stationary bike,'" Beardsley recalled. The new stationary bike could help him keep in shape during the coming cold Upper Midwest winter. His son sounded upbeat.

"That day before, there wasn't a clue," he said. "I don't know what hit him.

"I can't imagine a human going through anything more difficult," he said, fighting back tears. "That makes everything else that has happened seem like a walk in the park. I think about him all the time.

"We still question what more we could have done. I know he is a much better place. That brings me joy."

These days, Beardsley runs an inn with his wife, Jill, gives motivational talks for businesses, and works as a fishing guide. He runs races along Detroit Lake, Minnesota, including one named in honor of his son.

His speaking schedule includes appearances at mental health conferences, talking with those in similar situations. He values those conversations with other families.

"I look at it that at least Andy's death isn't in vain," he said. "Hopefully it will prevent others from doing what Andy did."

Losing on Purpose

MIKE PESCA

With apologies to Tolstoy, all winning teams are alike, but every loser loses in their own way.

Every winning team believes itself to have been resilient. To have "all bought in." To have come together as a family, and to have picked each other up when they were down. Every winning team was counted out at some point.

"No one expected us to fulfill this," Michael Jordan said after his Chicago Bulls won the 1998 NBA Finals. The Bulls, it should be noted, opened the season in Las Vegas as more likely to win the title than every other NBA team combined, never trailed in any playoff series, and had a roster that boasted a Hall of Fame coach, three Hall of Fame players in their primes, and, as Michael Jordan no doubt was aware of, Michael Jordan.

But the losers. Well, some flail. Some come apart at the seams, some have a culture of complacency, some lack the right mind-set. Some never gel. Some are blown out. Or, paradoxically even worse, come so close they can taste it, only to be left lapping at the dust of their rivals.

So many varieties of loser, yet one is rarest of all, and perhaps most disturbing. There is the type of loser that has the specific intention of playing the game in direct opposition to the supposed goals. I'm not speaking of a competitor who's been bought off, or a team that is "tanking" in order to get a better draft pick—an effort orchestrated by management, not the players on the floor. I'm talking about the rare occasion when all the incentives line up to lose a specific game, or help their opponent achieve their goals in a portion of a game, in an act that is both rational and disorienting to our instincts for fair play.

It turns out that sometimes winning in the end requires losing along the way.

BY THE TIME the last home game for the 1992 Yankees rolled around, the season was a lost cause. Seven games under .500, and sixteen and a half games out of first place in their division. All that was left for the Bronx Bombers was to close out another desultory year and ponder ways to get promising young outfielder Bernie Williams more at bats. On that temperate September day, they were playing the Toronto Blue Jays, who had a small lead in the division.

Four innings in the game was all but over; the Jays built up a 9–0 lead, giving pitcher Jack Morris a chance to become the first twenty-game-winning pitcher in franchise history.

But when rain began coming down in the top of the fifth inning, the Yankees saw an opening. If the game did not go five full innings, as per MLB rules, the Yankees could earn a rain delay, and perhaps a weather suspension, wiping their deficit off the books.

For the Blue Jays the exact opposite was true: the sooner they could close out the fifth inning, the better. In their case, playing for three quick outs was the optimal strategy for winning. With this in mind the Blue Jays' ninth batter, Alfredo Griffin, came to the plate. He aimed to whiff. On the mound for the Yankees was Greg Cadaret. He aimed to issue a walk. What if a hitter who won't hit meets a hurler who loses all interest in competently pitching?

Strike one provided an answer. Because Griffin did swing, mightily and from his heels, a breeze-inducing cut that ripped through the air with no care or attention paid to the pitch, which was actually in the vicinity of the strike zone. With this caricature of a swing, Griffin seemed to clue Cadaret in to the stakes involved. Pitch number two was delivered into the dirt to even the count at 1-1. What this insured was a kind of gentleman's agreement to make a mockery of baseball tradition. Cadaret began treating the strike zone like a cat treats a bathtub. But Griffin was having none of the all-but-intentional walk; he swung at balls out of the strike zone and balls wayyy out of the strike zone. The last pitch of this exchange was something of a classic of the genre. With the count 1-2 Cadaret delivered a pitch high above his catcher's glove. Griffin, however, was uninterested in hitability. He swung. Loopily, goofily, comically, purists would say afterward, farcically. This was the third strike. But, as the pitch had not been caught cleanly, the defense would have to tag the batter or throw the ball to first, the latter of which catcher Matt Nokes did. Yankees first baseman Don Mattingly caught the ball but then refused to step on the bag. Griffin took off—not toward the base, but into the dugout. The game was at an impasse. A team attempting to make an out met a defense that refused to allow them to do so.

Yankees manager Buck Showalter charged the field to protest and umpire John Shulock rendered a Solomonic verdict. The batter would be out, but the game would be suspended. Two and a half hours later it would resume, and the Yankees would humbly succumb to the Blue Jays.

Afterward Showalter said that he and Shulock were in agreement that the game should not be turned into a farce. When presented with this interpretation Griffin shouted, "I make a farce of the game?" He went on to ask, "They have to get me out anyway. Why is that a farce?"

Griffin, who later claimed he deployed his kamikaze tactics without input or instruction from manager Cito Gasten, was technically correct. Atypical spectacle and adherence to baseball's famed unwritten code aside, Griffin engaged in the proper winning strategy in that moment. By trying to lose he showed a winner's mentality and a champion's savvy.

The same is true for a group of women badminton players during the 2012 Olympic Games, but their sport came to view them with less charity.

THE BADMINTON BRACKETS at the London Games were dominated, as badminton often is, by a small group of nations. Since badminton became an official sport in the 1992 Games, the Indonesians, South Koreans, and Chinese athletes have dominated the women's doubles tournament. This was the case in London, where, with the round-robin rounds almost over, teams from China, South Korea, and both teams from Indonesia had already clinched spots in the tournament's knockout round. It became apparent to the Chinese that, in their last match in the first round, a loss would be more advantageous than a win for determining the best matchup in the next round. Unfortunately for them, and fans of norms of sportsmanship within the Olympic community, the South Korean team realized the same thing. Shuttlecock shenanigans ensued.

As China faced South Korea on the courts of Wembley Arena, the Chinese were trying to avoid meeting the *other* Chinese team before the knockout round; the South Koreans were also looking to lose. This gave rise to the spectacle of some of the top athletes in their sport serving birdie after birdie into the net, chasing down shots as if they were arthritic pensioners, and lobbing return shots far wide of the court. This wasn't the only match to draw raised eyebrows and then full-throated boos. In a later match, the Indonesians and a second team from South Korea performed this pathetic dance and did not perform it well. Threatened with black cards and regaled with the lusty jeers of a crowd, which obviously felt that each player was guilty of "conducting oneself in a manner that is clearly abusive or detrimental to the sport," the Badminton World Federation would eventually disqualify all eight players, using those exact words. (A new format was introduced in 2016, disguising knockout-round matchups, thereby eliminating the incentives for losing in the preliminary rounds.)

IDEALS OF SPORTSMANSHIP also came into conflict with a strange set of rules in 1994 during an international soccer tournament called the Shell Caribbean Cup (sponsored by the Petroleum company Royal Dutch Shell, not named for invertebrate exoskeletons scattered through the region's beaches). Group 1 consisted of three teams: Barbados, Grenada, and Puerto Rico. The final match of the three that were to be played pitted Barbados against Grenada with the following circumstances governing advancement to the next round: If Grenada won, they would be through. But Barbados needed to win by at least two goals to overcome their goal differential deficit.

This would be a fairly common situation in soccer, but for the odd rule that any goals scored in overtime period would count as two goals. Weird. But those were the rules.

The teams found themselves in the eighty-third minute with Barbados holding a 2–1 lead, meaning they had seven minutes plus stoppage time to score on Grenada, no easy task. But what would be a far easier task, in fact a certain one, would be for Barbados to score on themselves, force extra time, and put themselves in position to net one of those wacky two-point overtime goals.

Barbados went for it, stunning the confused Grenadians by purposefully equalizing with a couple of minutes left to play. Then the Grenadians got it, and realized that if they could score, either on their opponents or on *themselves*, the Barbadians would be eliminated from the tournament.

These backward incentives imposed a new set of rules on a very old game. It looked like soccer, but with one wrinkle—one team, Grenada, was desperate to score on either goal. The Barbadians played defense for the full length of the pitch, knowing that if the Grenadians simply lofted a kick into their own goal area their keeper could leap to catch the ball and throw it into his own goal. Somehow this game of Caribbean keep-away worked out for Barbados. They did reach extra time with the score tied at two, and during that period they scored one of those two-point goals the tournament organizers had invented, winning the match 4–2. Calling the end of regulation a "madhouse" Grenada manager James Clarkson argued after the match, "In football, you are supposed to score against the opponents to win, not for them."

ALL THESE INSTANCES were characterized by a wild deviation from the norms of play, deviations described by losing managers or Olympic officials as embarrassing, farcical, or in contradiction to the spirit of competition. Yet it was a dedication to competition, mixed with the ability to spot an advantage, that gave rise to all these unorthodox acts. It's as if the rule makers could not be bothered to sufficiently think through the consequences of their rules, but were all too happy to fall back on an unstated code of conduct as cover for the inadequacies that they created.

Though the athletes or teams who tried to lose on purpose were all accused of unethical behavior, that's a stretch. The more pertinent lesson is that it's hard to tamp down the drive of an intense competitor, harder still to require a top athlete to ignore self-interest as a cover for the mistakes of rule makers. Once norms of playing the game are violated you're sure to hear lectures about sportsmanship, but postgame shaming is no match for the dedicated athlete's desire to win, even if he or she has to lose a little to get there.

Larry and the Ball

ABBY ELLIN

The savior of my youth, the man who restored dignity to a hapless ball player—and thousands of despondent fans in the process—is not John Henry, Theo Epstein, Alex Cora, or any of the men responsible for finally bringing a World Series title to my beloved Red Sox. It's not even someone with a sports background. No, the person who redeemed a beleaguered first baseman is a neurotic, balding germaphobe named David.

Larry David.

Yes. That Larry David. The misanthropic mastermind behind *Seinfeld*, *Curb Your Enthusiasm*, and *SNL*'s version of Bernie Sanders; the astute observer about the world we inhabit. (A typical Larryism: "What is this compulsion to have people over at your house and serve them food and talk to them?")

To fully comprehend my gratitude to L.D., you have to

understand my history with the Red Sox, which dates back to the 1975 World Series: the Sox versus the Cincinnati Reds.

It was October, and I was sitting in the bleachers at Fenway Park with Danny Schiff, flirting like the eight-year-olds we were. Real flirting. True flirting. The most honest flirting there is. I'd gotten braces earlier that day and kept running my tongue over the metal. It felt strange to me, but I wasn't embarrassed. I grinned widely any time Danny glanced at me, my braces gleaming in the floodlights. It didn't occur to me to be embarrassed. I was cocksure and defiant, and exactly where I wanted to be: surrounded by my boys on a cool autumn night. With neither of our parents in sight.

And they *were* my boys, those 70s' ball players: Rick Burleson and Carlton "Pudge" Fisk and Dewey Evans and Jim Rice and Fred Lynn and Carl Yastrzemski. *Yaz!* For some inexplicable reason, my third-grade teacher brought in a plastic swimming pool and liberated a pack of crayfish into the water. We students got to pick one as a pet and name it. Mine, the biggest, was called Yaz. Crayfish make lousy pets, but Yaz was cool, with a splotch of pink nail polish on his shell, so we could identify him in a lineup.

But my real hero was Luis Tiant Jr., the great Cuban pitcher. (I would have named my crayfish for him, but Danny Schiff beat me to it.) One afternoon Tiant showed up outside the school gym with an older man who looked just like him. It was his father, Luis Senior. A bunch of us surrounded them and Tiant signed the slips of paper we handed him. But as my own father pointed out later on, it was Luis Senior who was the real star. He had also been a pitcher, but he wasn't allowed to play in the Major League Baseball organization because of his skin color. This was the first I'd heard about that, and it hurt my stomach.

The Sox lost the Series in seven games, and at the end of fourth grade Danny and his family moved to Houston. I never heard from him again, and the Sox never gave us much reason to celebrate. For the remainder of my childhood, the Red Sox never made it into another World Series.

Then, 1986.

That year, I was a sophomore at a small college in upstate New York. It was cold and bleak and I didn't want to be there. What I really wanted to do was take a year off after high school to find myself (or, ideally, someone else), but my parents squashed that idea like a pesky crustacean.

The confident girl of eight had been replaced by an angsty and angry eighteen-year-old. I couldn't connect with my peers for many reasons, not least of which that they were Yankee and Mets fans. I was miserable and lonely.

And yet . . . something good did happen: eleven years after my night in the bleachers with Danny Schiff, the Red Sox were headed back to the World Series.

I didn't want to watch the games with these misguided New Yorkers; I wanted to be in Boston with my people. But I latched onto a handful of New Englanders also stuck behind enemy lines. By Game 6, we were feeling pretty good.

It didn't last. Oh, boy did it not last. Like all of America, we witnessed one of baseball's Greatest Tragedies, involving a ground ball, first base, and feet spread a little too far apart. As the ball rolled through the first baseman's legs—his name was Bill Buckner—everyone around me yelped as if they'd smacked headfirst into the Green Monster. My own feelings ranged from rage to pity to despair. It was as if we'd watched a suicide in real time—which, in effect, we had. For the next few days the campus was littered with conversations about Buckner's error: in classes, at meals, in the dorms. No one could shut up about it.

I needed to flee.

So when a guy I barely knew asked me if I wanted to road-trip to New York City in his brand-new BMW, I jumped. He said something about a ticker-tape parade, but I had no idea what that really was. Why would I? My team had never been given one, at least not in my lifetime. It sounded like fun: A parade! With confetti! I didn't realize that this wasn't like Times Square on New Year's Eve, when everyone celebrated in unison around a shared event. This was something for a very specific audience—one I was emphatically not a part of. Of course, I wouldn't know this until we grabbed the 1 train to lower Manhattan, smushed between 64.8 tons of falling orange and blue paper and people celebrating—nay, *reveling*—in the catastrophe that befell my Red Sox.

"Orosco!" the fans hooted. "Ohh-RAWWWW—sco!"

I stood there, my teeth clenched, my lips pressed into a hostile line. "Boo!" I yelled. "Boo!"

Everyone turned to me, eyes blazing at the traitor in their midst. I was lucky to make it out alive.

THE RED SOX EVENTUALLY broke the Curse in 2004 and 2007 and 2013 and 2018. But thirty-three years after the Gaffe Seen Round the World, Buckner was still greeted with derision. His name was both a euphemism and a verb, and not a happy one like, say, "to kiss."

Then episode 9, season 8, of *Curb Your Enthusiasm* came along. The "Mister Softee" episode, 2011. And everything changed.

BECAUSE IT IS LARRY DAVID, everything is always convoluted and weird, but this episode is especially so. It involves a softball game in Central Park, and a ball rolling through the first baseman's legs—Larry David's legs. It's not his fault, not really: he's distracted by the Mister Softee jingle emanating from an ice cream truck whizzing past, and it catapults him back to his own childhood. Back then, poor Larry, his Jewfro at full mast, is on the losing side of a strip poker game played inside of an ice cream truck. Fifty years later, he's still traumatized by the relentless music. He can't be held accountable for his error.

The team owner is apoplectic. "YOU BUCKNERED IT!" he screams. "You fucking Bucknered it!"

Larry shrugs. *Shit happens.*

A few hours later, Larry attends a sports paraphernalia event to buy a gift for his manager, Jeff Greene: a baseball autographed by Mookie Wilson, the Met who lobbed the ball that Buckner missed.

Buckner is also at the event. He and Larry start talking and decide to have lunch. Everywhere they go—even on the streets of Manhattan—people taunt them.

"Fuck you, Buckner! You stink!"

"Don't let the door go through your legs on the way out, Buckner!"

Larry brings Buckner over to Jeff's apartment, so he can give him the signed baseball.

As Buckner stands at the open window and admires the view, Larry tosses him the ball. Buckner misses and it flies outside.

"I thought you were a baseball player!" Jeff's wife, Susie, shrieks. "You can't catch a goddamn toss?"

"Shit happens," Buckner says, shrugging.

Later that day, Larry happens upon a burning apartment building. A woman and her baby are trapped on a top floor. The firefighters set up a rubber tarp, and the woman is supposed to chuck her baby out the window.

She takes a deep breath and flings her child into the ether. He falls, in slow motion, onto the rubber. But instead of landing, he bounces again, soaring high, high into the air. Coincidentally, Buckner is staying at a hotel around the corner, and he strolls by this seismic event. He leaps into action, arms outstretched, lurching toward the baby. Terror is etched onto everyone's faces; they knew who this man is. He can't catch a ball for shit, let alone a kid.

But then, hallelujah! Buckner flies into the air, arms outstretched, and catches the bouncing child. Buckner stumbles onto the ground but he clutches that baby to his breast, smiling broadly. The crowd—a New York crowd—roars! It's the World Series and the ticker-tape parade rolled into one. Buckner is hoisted onto someone's shoulders, brandished as if he's the Commissioner's Trophy.

Buckens beams. He finally gets the reception that should have been his thirty-three years ago.

I weep.

I WEEP AGAIN, seven years later, when my Twitter feed blows up: Bill Buckner has died. The pundits and columnists once again dissect the series; in retrospect, maybe Buckner wasn't so bad, kinda like Nixon. After all, the Sox wouldn't have even made it to the World Series without his help. The dude had a stellar record.

It's a nice sentiment, but a little too late. Buckner doesn't need it anymore. He was redeemed in the most brilliant way possible.

The Loser

GAY TALESE

At the foot of a mountain in upstate New York, about 60 miles from Manhattan, there is an abandoned country clubhouse with a dusty dance floor, upturned barstools, and an untuned piano; and the only sounds heard around the place at night come from the big white house behind it—the clanging sounds of garbage cans being toppled by raccoons, skunks, and stray cats making their nocturnal raids down from the mountain.

The white house seems deserted, too; but occasionally, when the animals become too clamorous, a light will flash on, a window will open, and a Coke bottle will come flying through the darkness and smash against the cans. But mostly the animals are undisturbed until daybreak, when the rear door of the white house swings open and a broad-shouldered Negro appears in gray sweat clothes with a white towel around his neck.

He runs down the steps, quickly passes the garbage cans,

and proceeds at a trot down the dirt road beyond the country club toward the highway. Sometimes he stops along the road and throws a flurry of punches at imaginary foes, each jab punctuated by hard gasps of his breathing—"*hegh-hegh-hegh*"—and then, reaching the highway, he turns and soon disappears up the mountain.

At this time of morning, farm trucks are on the road, and the drivers wave at the runner. And later in the morning, other motorists see him, and a few stop suddenly at the curb and ask:

"Say, aren't *you* Floyd Patterson?"

"No," says Floyd Patterson, "I'm his brother, Raymond."

The motorists move on, but recently a man on foot, a disheveled man who seemed to have spent the night outdoors, staggered behind the runner along the road and yelled, "Hey, Floyd Patterson!"

"No, I'm his brother, Raymond."

"Don't tell *me* you're not Floyd Patterson. I know what Floyd Patterson looks like."

"Okay," Patterson said, shrugging, "if you want me to be Floyd Patterson, I'll be Floyd Patterson."

"So let me have your autograph," said the man, handing him a rumpled piece of paper and a pencil.

He signed it—"Raymond Patterson."

One hour later Floyd Patterson was jogging his way back down the dirt path toward the white house, the towel over his head absorbing the sweat from his brow. He lives alone in a two-room apartment in the rear of the house, and has remained there in almost complete seclusion since getting knocked out a second time by Sonny Liston.

In the smaller room is a large bed he makes up himself, several record albums he rarely plays, a telephone that seldom rings. The larger room has a kitchen on one side and, on the other, adjacent to a sofa, is a fireplace from which are hung boxing trunks and T-shirts to dry, and a photograph of him when he was the champion, and also a television set. The set is usually on except when Patterson is sleeping, or when he is sparring across the road inside the clubhouse (the ring is rigged over what was once the dance floor), or when, in a rare moment of painful honesty, he reveals to a visitor what it is like to be the loser.

"Oh, I would give up anything to just be able to work with Liston, to box with him somewhere where nobody would see us, and to see if I could get past three minutes with him," Patterson was saying, wiping his face with the towel, pacing slowly around the room near the sofa. "I *know* I can do better. . . . Oh, I'm not talking about a rematch. Who would pay a nickel for another Patterson-Liston fight? I know *I* wouldn't. . . . But all I want to do is get past the first round."

Then he said, "You have no idea how it is in the first round. You're out there with all those people around you, and those cameras, and the whole world looking in, and all that movement, that excitement, and 'The Star-Spangled Banner,' and the whole nation hoping you'll win, including the President. And do you know what all this does? It blinds you, just blinds you. And then the bell rings, and you go at

Liston and he's coming at you, and you're not even aware that there's a referee in the ring with you.

". . . Then you can't remember much of the rest, because you don't want to. . . . All you recall is, all of a sudden you're getting up, and the referee is saying, 'You all right?' and you say, 'Of *course* I'm all right,' and he says, 'What's your name?' and you say, 'Patterson.'

"And then, suddenly, with all this screaming around you, you're down again, and you know you have to get up, but you're extremely groggy, and the referee is pushing you back, and your trainer is in there with a towel, and people are all standing up, and your eyes focus directly at no one person—you're sort of floating.

"It is not a *bad* feeling when you're knocked out," he said. "It's a *good* feeling, actually. It's not painful, just a sharp grogginess. You don't see angels or stars; you're on a pleasant cloud. After Liston hit me in Nevada, I felt, for about four or five seconds, that everybody in the arena was actually in the ring with me, circled around me like a family, and you feel warmth toward all the people in the arena after you're knocked out. You feel lovable to all the people. And you want to reach out and kiss everybody—men and women—and after the Liston fight, somebody told me I actually blew a kiss to the crowd from the ring. I don't remember that. But I guess it's true because that's the way you feel during the four or five seconds after a knockout. . . .

"But then," Patterson went on, still pacing, "this good feeling leaves you. You realize where you are, and what you're doing there, and what has just happened to you. And what follows is a hurt, a confused hurt—not a physical hurt—it's a hurt combined with anger; it's a what-will-people-think hurt; it's an ashamed-of-my-own-ability hurt. . . . And all you want then is a hatch door in the middle of the ring—a hatch door that will open and let you fall through and land in your dressing room instead of having to get out of the ring and face those people. The worst thing about losing is having to walk out of the ring and face those people. . . ."

Then Patterson walked over to the stove and put on the kettle for tea. He remained silent for a few moments. Through the walls could be heard the footsteps and voices of the sparring partners and the trainer who live in the front of the house. Soon they would be in the clubhouse getting things ready should Patterson wish to spar. In two days he was scheduled to fly to Stockholm and fight an Italian named Amonti, Patterson's first appearance in the ring since the last Liston fight.

Next he hoped to get a fight in London against Henry Cooper. Then, if his confidence was restored, his reflexes reacting, Patterson hoped to start back up the ladder in this country, fighting all the leading contenders, fighting often, and not waiting so long between each fight as he had done when he was a champion in the 90-percent tax bracket.

His wife, whom he finds little time to see, and most of his friends think he should quit. They point out that he does not need the money. Even he admits that, from investments alone on his $8,000,000 gross earning, he should have an annual income of about $35,000 for the next 25 years. But

Patterson, who is only 29 years old and barely scratched, cannot believe that he is finished. He cannot help but think that it was something more than Liston that destroyed him—a strange, psychological force was also involved, and unless he can fully understand what it was, and learn to deal with it in the boxing ring, he may never be able to live peacefully anywhere but under this mountain. Nor will he ever be able to discard the false whiskers and moustache that, ever since Johansson beat him in 1959, he has carried with him in a small attaché case into each fight so he can slip out of the stadium unrecognized should he lose.

"I often wonder what other fighters feel, and what goes through their minds when they lose," Patterson said, placing the cups of tea on the table. "I've wanted so much to talk to another fighter about all this, to compare thoughts, to see if he feels some of the same things I've felt. But who can you talk to? Most fighters don't talk much anyway. And I can't even look another fighter in the eye at a weigh-in, for some reason.

"At the Liston weigh-in, the sports writers noticed this, and said it showed I was afraid. But that's not it. I can never look *any* fighter in the eye because . . . well, because we're going to fight, which isn't a nice thing, and because . . . well, once I actually did look a fighter in the eye. It was a long, long time ago. I must have been in the amateurs then. And when I looked at this fighter, I saw he had such a nice face . . . and then he looked at *me* . . . and *smiled* at me . . . and *I* smiled back! It was strange, very strange. When a guy can look at another guy and smile like that, I don't think they have any business fighting.

"I don't remember what happened in that fight, and I don't remember what the guy's name was. I only remember that, ever since, I have never looked another fighter in the eye."

The telephone rang in the bedroom. Patterson got up to answer it. It was his wife, Sandra. So he excused himself, shutting the bedroom door behind him.

Sandra Patterson and their four children live in a $100,000 home in an upper-middle-class white neighborhood in Scarsdale, New York. Floyd Patterson feels uncomfortable in this home surrounded by a manicured lawn and stuffed with furniture, and, since losing his title to Liston, he has preferred living full time at his camp, which his children have come to know as "Daddy's house." The children, the eldest of whom is a daughter named Jeannie now seven years old, do not know exactly what their father does for a living. But Jeannie, who watched the last Liston-Patterson fight on closed-circuit television, accepted the explanation that her father performs in a kind of game where the men take turns pushing one another down; he had his turn pushing them down, and now it is their turn.

The bedroom door opened again, and Floyd Patterson, shaking his head, was very angry and nervous.

"I'm not going to work out today," he said. "I'm going to fly down to Scarsdale. These boys are picking on Jeannie again. She's the only Negro in this school, and the older kids give her a rough time, and some of the older boys tease her and lift up her dress all the time. Yesterday she went home crying, and so today I'm going down there and plan to wait outside the school for those boys to come out, and . . ."

"How old are they?" he was asked.

"Teen-agers," he said. "Old enough for a left hook."

Patterson telephoned his pilot friend, Ted Hanson, who stays at the camp and does public-relations work for him, and has helped teach Patterson to fly. Five minutes later Hanson, a lean white man with a crew cut and glasses, was knocking on the door; and ten minutes later both were in the car that Patterson was driving almost recklessly over the narrow, winding country roads toward the airport, about six miles from the camp.

"Sandra is afraid I'll cause trouble; she's worried about what I'll do to those boys, she doesn't want trouble!" Patterson snapped, swerving around a hill and giving his car more gas. "She's just not firm enough! She's afraid . . . she was afraid to tell me about that groceryman who's been making passes at her. It took her a long time before she told me about that dishwasher repairman who comes over and calls her 'baby.' They all know I'm away so much. And that dishwasher repairman has been to my home about four five times this month already. That machine breaks down every week. I guess he fixes it so it breaks down every week. Last time, I laid a trap. I waited forty-five minutes for him to come, but then he didn't show up. I was going to grab him and say, 'How would you like it if I called *your* wife *baby*? You'd feel like punching me in the nose, wouldn't you? Well, that's what I'm going to do—if you ever call her *baby* again. You call her Mrs. Patterson; or Sandra, if you know her. But you don't know her, so call her Mrs. Patterson.' And then I told Sandra that these men, this type of white man, he just wants to have some fun with colored women. He'll never marry a colored woman, just wants to have some fun. . . ."

Now he was driving into the airport's parking lot. Directly ahead, roped to the grass airstrip, was the single-engine green Cessna that Patterson bought and learned to fly before the second Liston fight. Flying was a thing Patterson had always feared—a fear shared, maybe inherited from, his manager, Cus D'Amato, who still will not fly.

D'Amato, who took over training Patterson when the fighter was 17 or 18 years old and exerted a tremendous influence over his psyche, is a strange but fascinating man of fifty-six who is addicted to Spartanism and self-denial and is possessed by suspicion and fear; he avoids subways because he fears someone might push him onto the tracks; never has married; never reveals his home address.

"I must keep my enemies confused," D'Amato once explained. "When they are confused, then I can do a job for my fighters. What I do not want in life, however, is a sense of security; the moment a person knows security, his senses are dulled—and he begins to die. I also do not want many pleasures in life; I believe the more pleasure you get out of living, the more fear you have of dying."

Until a few years ago, D'Amato did most of Patterson's talking, and ran things like an Italian *padrone*. But later

Patterson, the maturing son, rebelled against the Father Image. After losing to Sonny Liston the first time—a fight D'Amato had urged Patterson to resist—Patterson took flying lessons. And before the second Liston fight, Patterson had conquered his fear of height, was master at the controls, was filled with renewed confidence—and knew, too, that, even if he lost, he at least possessed a vehicle that could get him out of town fast.

But it didn't. After the fight, the little Cessna, weighed down by too much luggage, became overheated ninety miles outside of Las Vegas. Patterson and his pilot companion, having no choice but to turn back, radioed the airfield and arranged for the rental of a larger plane. When they landed, the Vegas air terminal was filled with people leaving town after the fight. Patterson hid in the shadow behind a hangar. His beard was packed in the trunk. But nobody saw him.

Later the pilot flew Patterson's Cessna back to New York alone. And Patterson flew in the larger, rented plane. He was accompanied on this flight by Hanson, a friendly, forty-two-year-old, thrice divorced Nevadan who once was a crop duster, a bartender, and a cabaret hoofer; later he became a pilot instructor in Las Vegas, and it was there that he met Patterson. The two became good friends. And when Patterson asked Hanson to help fly the rented plane back to New York, Hanson did not hesitate, even though he had a slight hangover that night—partly due to being depressed by Liston's victory, partly due to being slugged in a bar by a drunk after objecting to some unflattering things the drunk had said about the fight.

Once in the airplane, however, Ted Hanson became very alert; he had to, because, after the plane had cruised a while at 10,000 feet, Floyd Patterson's mind seemed to wander back to the ring, and the plane would drift off course, and Hanson would say, "Floyd, Floyd, how's about getting back on course?" and then Patterson's head would snap up and his eyes would flash toward the dials. And everything would be all right for a while. But then he was back in the arena, reliving the fight, hardly believing that it had really happened. . . .

". . . And I kept thinking, as I flew out of Vegas that night, of all those months of training before the fight, all the roadwork, all the sparring, all the months away from Sandra. . . . thinking of the time in camp when I wanted to stay up until eleven-fifteen P.M. *to watch a certain movie on 'The Late Show.' But I didn't because I had roadwork the next morning . . .*

". . . And I was thinking about how good I'd felt before the fight, as I lay on the table in the dressing room. I remember thinking, 'You're in excellent physical condition, you're in good mental condition—but are you vicious?' But you tell yourself, 'Viciousness is not important now, don't think about it now; a championship fight's at stake, and that's important enough and, who knows? maybe you'll get vicious once the bell rings.'

". . . And so you lay there trying to get a little sleep . . . but you're only in a twilight zone, half asleep, and you're interrupted every once in a while by voices out in the hall, some guy's yelling 'Hey, Jack,' or 'Hey, Al,' or 'Hey, get those four-rounders into the ring.' And when you hear that, you think, They're not ready

for you yet. So you lay there . . . and wonder, Where will I be tomorrow? Where will I be three hours from now? Oh, you think all kinds of thoughts, some thoughts completely unrelated to the fight . . . you wonder whether you ever paid your mother-in-law back for all those stamps she bought a year ago . . . and you remember that time at two A.M. when Sandra tripped on the steps while bringing a bottle up to the baby . . . and then you get mad and ask: What am I thinking about these things for? . . . and you try to sleep . . . but then the door opens and somebody says to somebody else, 'Hey, is somebody gonna go to Liston's dressing room to watch 'em bandage up?'

". . . And so then you know it's about time to get ready. . . . You open your eyes. You get off the table. You glove up, you loosen up. Then Liston's trainer walks in. He looks at you, he smiles. He feels the bandages and later he says, 'Good luck, Floyd,' and you think, He didn't have to say that, he must be a nice guy.

". . . And then you go out, and it's the long walk, always a long walk, and you think, What am I gonna be when I come back this way? Then you climb into the ring. You notice Billy Eckstine at ringside leaning over to talk to somebody, and you see the reporters—some you like, some you don't like—and then it's 'The Star-Spangled Banner,' and the cameras are rolling, and the bell rings. . . .

". . . How could the same thing happen twice? How? That's all I kept thinking after the knockout. . . . Was I fooling these people all these years? . . . Was I ever the champion? . . . And then they lead you out of the ring . . . and up the aisle you go,

past those people, and all you want is to get to your dressing room, fast . . . but the trouble was in Las Vegas they made a wrong turn along the aisle, and when we got to the end, there was no dressing room there . . . and we had to walk all the way back down the aisle, past the same people, and they must have been thinking, Patterson's not only knocked out, but he can't even find his dressing room. . . .

". . . In the dressing room I had a headache. Liston didn't hurt me physically—a few days later I only felt a twitching nerve in my teeth—it was nothing like some fights I've had: like that Dick Wagner fight in '53 when he beat my body so bad I was urinating blood for days. After the Liston fight, I just went into the bathroom, shut the door behind me and looked at myself in the mirror. I just looked at myself, and asked, What happened? and then they started pounding on the door, and saying 'Com'on out, Floyd, Com'on out; the press is here, Cus is here, com'on out, Floyd. . . .'

". . . And so I went out, and they asked questions, but what can you say? What you're thinking about is all those months of training, all the conditioning, all the depriving; and you think, I didn't have to run that extra mile, didn't have to spar that day, I could have stayed up that night in camp and watched 'The Late Show'. . . . I could have fought this fight tonight in no condition. . . ."

"Floyd, Floyd," Hanson had said, "let's get back on course. . . ."

Again Patterson would snap out of his reverie, and refocus on the omniscope, and get his flying under control. After landing in New Mexico, and then in Ohio, Floyd Patterson and Ted Hanson brought the little plane into the New York airstrip near the fight camp. The green Cessna that had been flown back by the other pilot was already there, roped to the grass at precisely the same spot it was on this day five months later when Floyd Patterson was planning to fly it toward perhaps another fight—this time a fight with some schoolboys in Scarsdale who had been lifting up his little daughter's dress.

Patterson and Ted Hanson untied the plane, and Patterson got a rag and wiped from the windshield the splotches of insects. Then he walked around behind the plane, inspected the tail, checked under the fuselage, then peered down between the wing and the flaps to make sure all the screws were tight. He seemed suspicious of something. D'Amato would have been pleased.

"If a guy wants to get rid of you," Patterson explained, "all he has to do is remove these little screws here. Then, when you try to come in for a landing, the flaps fall off, and you crash."

Then Patterson got into the cockpit and started the engine. A few moments later, with Hanson beside him, Patterson was racing the little plane over the grassy field, then soaring over the weeds, then flying high above the gentle hills and trees. It was a nice takeoff.

Since it was only a forty-minute flight to the Westchester airport, where Sandra Patterson would be waiting with a car, Floyd Patterson did all the flying. The trip was uneventful until, suddenly behind a cloud, he flew into heavy smoke that hovered above a forest fire. His visibility gone, he was forced to the instruments. And at this precise moment, a fly that had been buzzing in the back of the cockpit flew up front and landed on the instrument panel in front of Patterson. He glared at the fly, watched it crawl slowly up the windshield, then shot a quick smash with his palm against the glass. He missed. The fly buzzed safely past Patterson's ear, bounced off the back of the cockpit, circled around.

"This smoke won't keep up," Hanson assured. "You can level off."

Patterson leveled off.

He flew easily for a few moments. Then the fly buzzed to the front again, zigzagging before Patterson's face, landed on the panel, and proceeded to crawl across it. Patterson watched it, squinted. Then he slammed down at it with a quick right hand. Missed.

Ten minutes later, his nerves still on edge, Patterson began the descent. He picked up the radio microphone—"Westchester tower . . . Cessna 2729 uniform . . . three miles northwest . . . land in one-six on final . . ."—and then, after an easy landing, he climbed quickly out of the cockpit and strode toward his wife's station wagon outside the terminal.

But along the way a small man smoking a cigar turned toward Patterson, waved at him, and said, "Say, excuse me, but aren't you . . . aren't you . . . Sonny Liston?"

Patterson stopped. He glared at the man, bewildered. He wasn't sure whether it was a joke or an insult, and he really did not know what to do.

"Aren't you Sonny Liston?" the man repeated, quite serious.

"No," Patterson said, quickly passing by the man. "I'm his brother."

When he reached Mrs. Patterson's car, he asked, "How much time till school lets out?"

"About fifteen minutes," she said, starting up the engine. Then she said, "Oh, Floyd, I just should have told Sister, I shouldn't have . . ."

"*You* tell Sister; *I'll* tell the boys. . . ."

Mrs. Patterson drove as quickly as she could into Scarsdale, with Patterson shaking his head and telling Ted Hanson in the back, "Really can't understand these school kids. This is a religious school, and they want $20,000 for a glass window—and yet, some of them carry these racial prejudices, and it's mostly the Jews who are shoulder to shoulder with us, and . . ."

"Oh, Floyd," cried his wife, "Floyd, *I* have to get along here . . . you're not here, *you* don't live here, I . . ."

She arrived at the school just as the bell began to ring. It was a modern building at the top of a hill, and on the lawn was the statue of a saint and, behind it, a large white cross.

"There's Jeannie," said Mrs. Patterson.

"Hurry, call her over here," Patterson said.

"Jeannie! Come over here, honey."

The little girl, wearing a blue school uniform and cap, and clasping books in front of her, came running down the path toward the station wagon.

"Jeannie," Floyd Patterson said, rolling down his window, "point out the boys who lifted your dress."

Jeannie turned and watched as several students came down the path; then she pointed to a tall, thin, curly-haired boy walking with four other boys, all about twelve to fourteen years of age.

"Hey," Patterson called to him, "can I see you for a minute?"

All five boys came to the side of the car. They looked Patterson directly in the eye. They seemed not at all intimidated by him.

"You the one that's been lifting up my daughter's dress?" Patterson asked the boy who had been singled out.

"Nope," the boy said, casually.

"Nope?" Patterson said, caught off guard by the reply.

"Wasn't him, Mister," said another boy. "Probably was his little brother."

Patterson looked at Jeannie. But she was speechless, uncertain. The five boys remained there, waiting for Patterson to do something.

"Well, er, where's your little brother?" Patterson asked.

"Hey, kid!" one of the boys yelled. "Come over here."

A boy walked toward them. He resembled his older brother; he had freckles on his small, upturned nose, had blue eyes, dark curly hair, and, as he approached the station wagon, he seemed equally unintimidated by Patterson.

"You been lifting up my daughter's dress?"

"Nope," the boy said.

"*Nope!*" Patterson repeated, frustrated.

"Nope, I wasn't lifting it. I was just touching it a little . . ."

The other boys stood around the car looking down at Patterson, and other students crowded behind them, and nearby Patterson saw several white parents standing next to their parked cars; he became self-conscious, began to tap nervously with his fingers against the dashboard. He could not raise his voice without creating an unpleasant scene, yet he could not retreat gracefully; so his voice went soft, and he said, finally:

"Look, boy, I want you to stop it. I won't tell your mother—that might get you in trouble—but don't do it again, okay?"

"Okay."

The boys calmly turned and walked, in a group, up the street. Sandra Patterson said nothing. Jeannie opened the door, sat in the front seat next to her father, and took out a small blue piece of paper that a nun had given her and handed it across to Mrs. Patterson. But Floyd Patterson snatched it. He read it. Then he paused, put the paper down, and quietly announced, dragging out the words, "*She didn't do her religion. . . .* "

Patterson now wanted to get out of Scarsdale. He wanted to return to camp. After stopping at the Patterson home in Scarsdale and picking up Floyd Patterson, Jr., who is three, Mrs. Patterson drove them all back to the airport. Jeannie and Floyd, Jr., were seated in the back of the plane, and then Mrs. Patterson drove the station wagon alone up to camp, planning to return to Scarsdale that evening with the children.

It was four P.M. when Floyd Patterson got back to the

camp, and the shadows were falling on the clubhouse, and on the tennis court routed by weeds, and on the big white house in front of which not a single automobile was parked. All was deserted and quiet; it was a loser's camp.

The children ran to play inside the clubhouse; Patterson walked slowly toward his apartment to dress for the workout.

"What could I do with those schoolboys?" he asked. "What can you do to kids of that age?"

It still seemed to bother him—the effrontery of the boys, the realization that he had somehow failed, the probability that, had those same boys heckled someone in Liston's family, the schoolyard would have been littered with limbs.

While Patterson and Liston both are products of the slum, and while both began as thieves, Patterson had been tamed in a special school with help from a gentle Negro spinster; later he became a Catholic convert, and learned not to hate. Still later he bought a dictionary, adding to his vocabulary such words as "vicissitude" and "enigma." And when he regained his championship from Johansson, he became the Great Black Hope of the Urban League.

He proved that it is not only possible to rise out of a Negro slum and succeed as a sportsman, but also to develop into an intelligent, sensitive, law-abiding citizen. In proving this, however, and in taking pride in it, Patterson seemed to lose part of himself. He lost part of his hunger, his anger—and as he walked up the steps into his apartment, he was saying, "I became the good guy. . . . After Liston won the title, I kept hoping that he would change into a good guy, too. That would have relieved me of the responsibility, and maybe I could have been more of the bad guy. But he didn't. . . . It's okay to be the good guy when you're winning. But when you're losing, it is no good being the good guy."

Patterson took off his shirt and trousers and, moving some books on the bureau to one side, put down his watch, his cuff links, and a clip of bills.

"Do you do much reading?" he was asked.

"No," he said. "In fact, you know I've never finished reading a book in my whole life? I don't know why. I just feel that no writer today has anything for me; I mean, none of them has felt any more deeply than I have, and I have nothing to learn from them. Although Baldwin to me seems different from the rest. What's Baldwin doing these days?"

"He's writing a play. Anthony Quinn is supposed to have a part in it."

"Quinn?" Patterson asked.

"Yes."

"Quinn doesn't like me."

"Why?"

"I read or heard it somewhere; Quinn had been quoted as saying that my fight was disgraceful against Liston, and Quinn said something to the effect that he could have done better. People often say that—*they* could have done better! Well, I think that if *they* had to fight, *they* couldn't even go through the experience of waiting for the fight to begin. They'd be up the whole night before, and would be drinking, or taking drugs. They'd probably get a heart attack. I'm sure that if I was in the ring with Anthony Quinn, I could wear him out without even touching him. I would do nothing but pressure him, I'd stalk him, I'd stand close to him. I wouldn't touch him, but I'd wear him out and he'd collapse. But Anthony Quinn's an old man, isn't he?"

"In his forties."

"Well, anyway," Patterson said, "getting back to Baldwin, he seems like a wonderful guy. I've seen him on television, and, before the Liston fight in Chicago, he came by my camp. You meet Baldwin on the street and you say, 'Who's this poor slob?'—he seems just like another guy; and this is the same impression *I* give people when they don't know me. But I think Baldwin and me, we have much in common, and someday I'd just like to sit somewhere for a long time and talk to him. . . ."

Patterson, his trunks and sweat pants on, bent over to tie his shoelaces, and then, from a bureau drawer, took out a T-shirt across which was printed "Deauville." He has several T-shirts bearing the same name. He takes good care of them. They are souvenirs from the high point of his life. They are from the Deauville Hotel in Miami Beach, which is where he trained for the third Ingemar Johansson match in March of 1961.

Never was Floyd Patterson more popular, more admired than during that winter. He had visited President Kennedy; he had been given a $35,000 jeweled crown by his manager; his greatness was conceded by sports writers—and nobody had any idea that Patterson, secretly, was in possession of a false moustache and dark glasses that he intended to wear out of Miami Beach should he lose the third fight to Johansson.

It was after being knocked out by Johansson in their first fight that Patterson, deep in depression, hiding in humiliation for months in a remote Connecticut lodge, decided he could not face the public again if he lost. So he bought false whiskers and a moustache, and planned to wear them out of his dressing room after a defeat. He had also planned, in leaving his dressing room, to linger momentarily within the crowd and perhaps complain out loud about the fight. Then he would slip undiscovered through the night and into a waiting automobile.

Although there proved to be no need for bringing disguise into the second or third Johansson fights, or into a subsequent bout in Toronto against an obscure heavyweight named Tom McNeeley, Patterson brought it anyway; and, after the first Liston fight, he not only wore it during his thirty-hour automobile ride from Chicago to New York, but he also wore it while in an airliner bound for Spain.

"As I got onto this plane, you'd never have recognized me," he said. "I had on this beard, moustache, glasses and hat—and I also limped, to make myself look older. I was alone. I didn't care what plane I boarded; I just looked up and saw this sign at the terminal reading 'Madrid,' and so I got on that flight after buying a ticket.

"When I got to Madrid I registered at a hotel under the name 'Aaron Watson.' I stayed in Madrid about four or five days. In the daytime I wandered around to the poorer sections of the city, limping, looking at the people, and the people stared back at me and must have thought I was crazy because I was moving so slow and looked the way I did. I ate food in my hotel room. Although once I went to a restaurant and ordered soup. I hate soup. But I thought it was what old people would order. So I ate it. And after a week of this, I began to actually think I was somebody else. I began to believe it. And it is nice, every once in a while, being somebody else."

Patterson would not elaborate on how he managed to register under a name that did not correspond to his passport; he merely explained, "With money, you can do anything."

Now, walking slowly around the room, his black silk robe over his sweat clothes, Patterson said, "You must wonder what makes a man do things like this. Well, I wonder, too. And the answer is, I don't know . . . but I think that within me, within every human being, there is a certain weakness. It is a weakness that exposes itself more when you're alone. And I have figured out that part of the reason I do the things I do, and cannot seem to conquer that one *word—myself—* is because . . . I am a coward. . . ."

He stopped. He stood very still in the middle of the room, thinking about what he had just said, probably wondering whether he should have said it.

"I am a coward," he then repeated, softly. "My fighting has little to do with that fact, though. I mean you can be a fighter—and a *winning* fighter—and still be a coward. I was probably a coward on the night I won the championship back from Ingemar. And I remember another night, long ago, back when I was in the amateurs, fighting this big, tremendous man named Julius Griffin. I was only a hundred fifty-three pounds. I was petrified. It was all I could do to cross the ring. And then he came at me, and moved close to me . . . and from then on I don't know anything. I have no idea what happened. Only thing I know is, I saw him on the floor. And later somebody said, 'Man, I never saw anything like it. You just jumped up in the air, and threw thirty different punches. . . ."

"When did you first think you were a coward?" he was asked.

"It was after the first Ingemar fight."

"How does one see this cowardice you speak of?"

"You see it when a fighter loses. Ingemar, for instance, is not a coward. When he lost the third fight in Miami, he was at a party later at the Fontainebleau. Had I lost, I couldn't have gone to that party. And I don't see how he did. . . ."

"Could Liston be a coward?"

"That remains to be seen," Patterson said. "We'll find out what he's like after somebody beats him, how he takes it. It's easy to do anything in victory. It's in defeat that a man reveals himself. In defeat I can't face people. I haven't the strength to say to people, 'I did my best, I'm sorry, and what not.'"

"Have you no hate left?"

"I have hated only one fighter," Patterson said. "And that was Ingemar in the second fight. I had been hating him for a whole year before that—not because he beat me in the first fight, but because of what he did after. It was all that boasting in public, and his showing off his right-hand punch on television, his thundering right, his 'toonder and lightning.' And I'd be home watching him on television, and *hating* him. It is a miserable feeling, hate. When a man hates, he can't have any peace of mind. And for one solid year I hated him because, after he took everything away from me, deprived me of everything I was, he *rubbed it in*. On the night of the second fight, in the dressing room, I couldn't wait until I got into the ring.

"When he was a little late getting into the ring, I thought, He's holding me up; he's trying to unsettle me—well, I'll get him!"

"Why couldn't you hate Liston in the second match?"

Patterson thought for a moment, then said, "Look, if Sonny Liston walked into this room now and slapped me in the face, then you'd see a fight. You'd see the fight of our life because, then, a principle would be involved. I'd forget he was a human being. I'd forget I was a human being. And I'd fight accordingly."

"Could it be, Floyd, that you made a mistake in becoming a prizefighter?"

"What do you mean?"

"Well, you say you're a coward; you say you have little capacity for hate; and you seemed to lose your nerve against those schoolboys in Scarsdale this afternoon. Don't you think you might have been better suited for some other kind of work? Perhaps a social worker, or . . ."

"Are you asking why I continue to fight?"

"Yes."

"Well," he said, not irritated by the question, "first of all, I love boxing. Boxing has been good to me. And I might just as well ask you the question: 'Why do you write?' Or, 'Do you retire from writing every time you write a bad story?' And as to whether I should have become a fighter in the first place, well, let's see how I can explain it. . . . Look, let's say you're a man who has been in an empty room for days and days without food . . . and then they take you out of that room and put you into another room where there's food hanging all over the place . . . and the first thing you reach for, you eat. When you're hungry, you're not choosy, and so I chose the thing that was closest to me. That was boxing. One day I just wandered into a gymnasium and boxed a boy. And I beat him. Then I boxed another boy. I beat him, too. Then I kept boxing. And winning. And I said, 'Here, finally, is something I can do!'

"Now I wasn't a sadist," he quickly added. "But I liked beating people because it was the only thing I could do. And whether boxing was a sport or not, I wanted to make it a sport because it was a thing I could succeed at. And what were the requirements? Sacrifice. That's all. To anybody who comes from the Bedford-Stuyvesant section of Brooklyn, sacrifice comes easy. And so I kept fighting, and one day I became heavyweight champion, and I got to know people like you. And you wonder how I can sacrifice, how I can deprive myself so much? You just don't realize where I've come from. You don't understand where I was when it began for me.

"In those days, when I was about eight years old, everything I got—I stole. I stole to survive, and I did survive, but I seemed to hate myself. My mother told me I used to point to a photograph of myself hanging in the bedroom and say, 'I don't like that boy!' One day my mother found three large X's scratched with a nail or something over that photograph of me. I don't remember doing it. But I do remember feeling like a parasite at home. I remember how awful I used to feel at night when my father, a longshoreman, would come home so tired that, as my mother fixed food before him, he would fall asleep at the table because he was that tired. I would always take his shoes off and clean his feet. That was my job. And I felt so bad because here I was, not going to school, doing nothing, just watching my father come home; and on Friday nights it was even worse. He would come home with his pay, and he'd put every nickel of it on the table so my mother could buy food for all the children. I never wanted to be around to see that. I'd run and hide. And then I decided to leave home and start stealing—and I did. And I would never come home unless I brought something that I had stolen. Once I remember I broke into a dress store and stole a whole mound of dresses, at two A.M., and here I was, this little kid, carrying all those dresses over the wall, thinking they were all the same size, my mother's size, and thinking the cops would never notice me walking down the street with all those dresses piled over my head. They did, of course. . . . I went to the Youth House. . . ."

Floyd Patterson's children, who had been playing outside all this time around the country club, now became restless and began to call him, and Jeannie started to pound on his door. So Patterson picked up his leather bag, which contained his gloves, his mouthpiece, and adhesive tape, and walked with the children across the path toward the clubhouse.

He flicked on the light switches behind the stage near the piano. Beams of amber streaked through the dimly lit room and flashed onto the ring. He took off his robe, shuffled his feet in the rosin, skipped rope, and then began to shadowbox in front of the spit-stained mirror, throwing out quick combinations of lefts, rights, lefts, rights, each jab followed by a "*hegh-hegh-hegh-hegh.*" Then, his gloves on, he moved to the punching bag in the far corner, and soon the room reverberated to his rhythmic beat against the bobbling bag—rat-tat-tat-*tetteta*, rat-tat-tat-*tetteta*-rat-tat-tat-*tetteta*-rat-*tat-tetteta!*

The children, sitting on pink leather chairs, moved from the bar to the fringe of the ring, watched him in awe, sometimes flinching at the force of his pounding against the leather bag.

And this is how they would probably remember him years from now: a dark, solitary, glistening figure punching in the corner of a forlorn spot at the bottom of a mountain where people once came to have fun—until the clubhouse because unfashionable, the paint began to peel, and Negroes were allowed in.

As Floyd Patterson continued to bang away with lefts and rights, his gloves a brown blur against the bag, his daughter slipped quietly off her chair and wandered past the ring into the other room. There, on the other side of the bar and beyond a dozen round tables, was the stage. She climbed onto the stage and stood behind a microphone, long dead, and cried out, imitating a ring announcer, "Ladieeees and gentlemen . . . tonight we present . . ."

She looked around, puzzled. Then, seeing that her little brother had followed her, she waved him up to the stage and began again: "Ladieees and gentlemen . . . tonight we present . . . *Floydie Patterson. . . .* "

Suddenly, the pounding against the bag in the other room stopped. There was silence for a moment. Then Jeannie, still behind the microphone and looking down at her brother, said,

"Floydie, come up here!"

"No," he said.

"Oh, come up here!"

"*No*," he cried.

Then Floyd Patterson's voice, from the other room, called: "Cut it out . . . I'll take you both for a walk in a minute."

He resumed punching—rat-tat-tat-*tetteta*—and they returned to his side. But Jeannie interrupted, asking, "Daddy, how come you sweating?"

"Water fell on me," he said, still pounding.

"Daddy," asked Floyd, Jr., "how come you spit water on the floor before?"

"To get it out of my mouth."

He was about to move over to the heavier punching bag when the sound of Mrs. Patterson's station wagon could be heard moving up the road.

Soon she was in Patterson's apartment cleaning up a bit, patting the pillows, washing the teacups that had been left in the sink. One hour later the family was having dinner together. They were together for two mere hours; then, at ten P.M., Mrs. Patterson washed and dried all of the dishes, and put the garbage out in the can—where it would remain until the raccoons and skunks got to it.

And then, after helping the children with their coats and walking out to the station wagon and kissing her husband good-bye, Mrs. Patterson began the drive down the dirt road toward the highway. Patterson waved once, and stood for a moment watching the taillights go, and then he turned and walked slowly back toward the house.

This piece was originally published in the March 1964 issue of Esquire.

Contributors

Ryan Bailey is an award-winning sports journalist from London, England. He covers soccer and tennis for Yahoo, Bleacher Report, and Eurosport. He always roots for the underdog.

Charles Bock is the author of the novels *Beautiful Children* and *Alice & Oliver*. He lives with his daughter in Brooklyn.

Carla Correa is a senior editor the *New York Times* who loves gymnastics. She previously worked at ESPN, *The Washington Post*, and *The Baltimore Sun*. She is originally from Connecticut and now lives in New York City.

Sir Arthur Conan Doyle (1859–1930) was a British writer and creator of the character Sherlock Holmes. Originally a physician, Doyle authored more than fifty short stories about Holmes, as well as novels, plays, and a variety of nonfiction works.

Abby Ellin is a former *New York Times* columnist. She is the author of *Duped* and *Teenage Waistland.* But her greatest achievement is naming Karamel Sutra for Ben and Jerry's.

Sam Graham-Felsen is the author of *Green*, a novel about an interracial friendship in early '90s Boston.

Kevin A. Hall loves his three children, his chosen and blood families, and is learning slowly but surely to love himself too. He lives in Auckland, New Zealand, with his big heart and his big dreams.

Louisa Hall is the author of the novels *Speak* and *Trinity.* She teaches creative writing at the University of Iowa.

Andy Lehren is a veteran of fourteen marathons, including five as a guide for a visually impaired runner. He was one of the guides who helped her to win the 2015 Boston Marathon for visually impaired female runners. A former *New York Times* reporter, where he contributed to a Pulitzer Prize–winning series, he is now a senior editor for NBC News, where he has won a Peabody, an Emmy, and other honors.

Stefanie Loh is the features editor at *The Seattle Times*, but was a sports writer through her first decade in journalism. Stef is drawn to stories that explain a person's "why" in life. She lives in Seattle with her wife, Lauren, and her labradoodle, Gryffindor.

James Andrew Miller is an award-winning journalist who has worked in politics, media, and entertainment in a career spanning more than twenty years. Miller is the author of the recently released *New York Times* bestselling book *Powerhouse.* Prior to that, he was the coauthor of the #1 *New York Times* bestseller *Those Guys Have All the Fun* and *Live From New York*, which was on the *New York Times* list for five months and was named by *Fortune* as one of the top seventy-five "Smartest Books We Know." His first book, *Running in Place*, was also a bestseller.

Barry Newman, a *Wall Street Journal* feature writer for forty-three years, was a foreign correspondent for two decades, in Southeast Asia, Western Europe, and Eastern Europe. *News to Me* is a collection of his stories with new essays on how he got them.

Matt Nissenbaum is a husband, father, OG New Yorker, and adopted Angeleno. He's also a former competitive dodgeball player and a big LA Rams fan.

Ryan O'Hanlon is a writer and editor living in Los Angeles. He publishes a twice-a-week newsletter about soccer called *No Grass in the Clouds*.

Mike Pesca is the editor of *Upon Further Review: The Greatest What-If's in Sports History*. He is host of the daily Slate podcast *The Gist*. For ten years he was a reporter for NPR, where he primarily covered sports. In addition to hosting *Wait, Wait, Don't Tell Me*, his work has been featured on *This American Life*, *Radiolab*, *Inside the NFL*, *Baseball Prospectus*, and *Basketball Prospectus.*

Rowan Ricardo Phillips is the author of three books of poetry, *The Ground*, *Heaven*, and *Living Weapon*. He is also the author of a work of literary criticism, *When Blackness Rhymes with Blackness*, and a work of nonfiction, *The Circuit: A Tennis Odyssey*. Phillips has been the recipient of a Whiting Writers' Award, a Guggenheim Fellowship, the Nicolás Guillén Outstanding Book Award, the PEN/Osterweil Prize for Poetry, the Anisfield-Wolf Book Award, the GLCA New Writers Award, and the PEN/ESPN Award for Literary Sportswriting. He lives in New York City and Barcelona.

Brian Platzer is the author of the novels *Bed-Stuy Is Burning* and *The Body Politic*, as well as the parenting book *The Homework Handbook*.

Joshua Prager is a writer in New York City. He is writing a book about *Roe v. Wade* and its plaintiff.

Bob Sullivan is an independent journalist and author of two *New York Times* bestsellers, *Gotcha Capitalism* and *Stop Getting Ripped Off*. He's also host of the podcast *So, Bob*, about the unintended consequences of technology.

Jeremy Taiwo is a three-time Team USA decathlete and 2016 Olympian. He is a film aficionado, a health and wellness advocate, and a big Harry Potter nerd. He is a native Washingtonian who currently lives in Seattle.

Gay Talese is the author of fourteen books and contributes to *The New Yorker*. He began his career in 1956 as a reporter for *The New York Times*, where he remained for ten years. He is married to Nan Talese, an editor and publisher who has her own imprint at Doubleday, and the couple have two daughters, Pamela, a painter, and Catherine, a photographer.

Acknowledgments

Mary and Louisa would like to thank the contributors to the collection, Ann Godoff, Casey Denis, and the rest of the fabulous team at Penguin.

Louisa would also like to thank Sarah Chalfant and Rebecca Nagel at the Wylie Agency, and especially her winsome family.

Mary would like to thank Deborah Schneider at ICM, and her dear friends and family with a shout out to Pedro Pilon.

Credits

“The Sporting House” by Charles Bock, copyright © Charles Bock. Reprinted by permission of the author.

“Yankees Strike” by Bob Sullivan, copyright © 2020 by Bob Sullivan.

“Banderillero” Barry Newman, copyright © Barry Newman. Reprinted by permission of the author.

“An Athens Odyssey Skips the Medal Mark” by Kevin Hall, copyright © 2020 by Kevin Hall.

“The Peanut Vendor and the Curse” by Samuel Graham-Felsen, copyright © 2020 by Samuel Graham-Felsen.

“That Loser Lebron” by Ryan O’Hanlon, copyright © 2020 by Ryan O’Hanlon.

“Two White Kids from New York Kicking Ass” by Brian Platzer, copyright © 2020 by Brian Platzer.

“Too Lucky in Love” by Joshua Prager, adapted from excerpt(s) from *The Echoing Green: The Untold Story of Bobby Thomson, Ralph Branca and the Shot Heard Round the World* by Joshua Prager, copyright © 2006 by Joshua Prager. Used by permission of Joshua Prager and Pantheon Books, an imprint of the Knopf Doubleday Publishing Group, a division of Penguin Random House LLC. All rights reserved.

“If You Can’t Beat ’Em” by Louisa Hall, copyright © 2020 by Louisa Hall.

"The Great Wimbledon FC Heist" by Ryan Bailey, copyright © 2020 by Ryan Bailey.

"Requiem for the Ivory Coast" by Rowan Ricardo Phillips, copyright © Rowan Ricardo Phillips. Reprinted by permission of the author.

"The 'Dewey Defeats Truman' of Sports" by James Andrew Miller, copyright © 2020 by James Andrew Miller.

"Chasing Ashton Eaton" by Jeremy Taiwo, as told to Stefanie Loh. Reprinted by permission of Stefanie Loh.

"Galieva-ed" by Carla Correa, copyright © 2020 by Carla Correa.

"The Kyrgios Enigma" by Louisa Thomas, copyright © Louisa Thomas. Reprinted by permission of the author.

"Tomato Can Blues" by Mary Pilon originally appeared in *The New York Times* on September 18, 2013, is copyright of *The New York Times* and used here by permission.

"Washington Generals Win!" by Matt Nissenbaum, copyright © 2020 by Matt Nissenbaum.

"The Guy Wearing a Hat" by Andy Lehren, copyright © 2020 by Andy Lehren.

"Losing on Purpose" by Mike Pesca, copyright © 2020 by Mike Pesca.

"Larry and the Ball" by Abby Ellin, copyright © 2020 by Abby Ellin.

"The Loser" by Gay Talese, copyright © Gay Talese. Reprinted by permission of the author.